I0160751

ISBN 9780692726105

For Sharon, Donna, Estella, and Danielle. Thank you for the inspiration and help. Without you, this book would not have been possible.

Table of Contents

Index

Ascension Journey – The Ascension journey references the process of raising your personal vibration. It is called a journey because there is no end. Once you start on this path, it continues to evolve.

Chakras – The energy centers throughout the human body. Most people know of the seven primary ones: Root, Sacral, Solar Plexus, Heart, Throat, Third Eye and Crown. Chakras are believed to be part of the subtle body, not the physical body, and as such, are the meeting points of the subtle (non-physical) energy channels in the subtle body through which the life force moves. Although these 7 are the most commonly known, the human body has hundreds of chakras throughout.

Downloads – The way in which higher intelligence enters our energy body and our conscious mind. This is always how our own energy is transmuted and raised. The downloads are believed to come from the Universe, and provide us with information which we need in order to ascend to a higher level.

Energetically Open – Someone who has connected to their intuition and has tapped in to that knowledge. They may be completely unaware of this fact, but they still experience the things that come with being aware of energy.

Guardians – These are beings which are created by the people they are guarding. They are internal projections of a defense system. These beings are good for the person they are protecting, but harmful for anyone who tries to access that individual psychically. They will allow someone entry if the person they are guarding gives explicit permission. They can cause physical and psychic damage to anyone who attempts to enter without permission.

Guides – These are energetic beings who have taken on the role of helping people navigate life with ease, by giving advice and options when asked. Their entire goal is to support you along your journey.

Higher Self - This is your highest energetic expression. You can think of this as the ultimate expression of your soul. Your higher self is the one ultimately in charge of the life path you have taken. It can give permission, or withhold it, based on the life path you have chosen regardless of your conscious self. Your higher self is ultimately concerned with your spiritual evolution.

Hitchhikers – These are spirits and / or ghosts who attach themselves to people in order to "leech" off their energy. They are usually found in places with lots of energy like bars, casinos, anywhere you find children and loud noises.

Light – This term generally refers to the light of God or the Universe. This can be accessed by connecting to that place where we all go when we pray. Generally when people are connecting to the Light and bringing it in, they are pulling the energy of love into their bodies.

Light Worker – Refers to someone who uses their abilities to help others using the Light in this lifetime. Someone who is connected to their healing abilities and internal guidance. Psychics, healers, channels, etc. fall under this umbrella.

Medicine People – People from indigenous cultures and tribes who were taught healing arts. They are tribal healers and use energy and herbal medicines.

Space Clearing - The use of energy and other items like burning of sage or the sound of bells in order to clear the energy of a room. Scientifically, when a negative event happens in a place positive ions are released into that space and will stay until they are cleared. Space clearing involves creating enough negative ions within that space to eliminate the positive ions which had been floating around. This generally makes the space feel much better.

Spirits – These can be ghosts or other entities of that sort which exist along side us.

Universe - This term is used as one of many to describe the eternal knowledge. It can also be referred to as God, Source, Spirit (different than the spirits listed above), your higher intelligence. There is no religious dogma necessarily associated with this term. It refers to whatever higher intelligence you may believe in, including your own higher self.

Are You Ready?

Stop judging and hang on tight!! Those are the best words of advice I can give to anyone who wants to tackle raising their vibrations (the energy which radiates way from you, sometimes known as your aura). Ascension journey, or Spiritual Awakening, refers to the conscious effort to raise one's personal vibrational frequency, and expand personal and spiritual growth. Judgement is one of the largest barriers to raising your vibrations. This includes your interpretations of every situation you encounter, the different stories you tell yourself about why things are the way they are, and comparing yourself to others along the journey. This book is the one I wish would have been available as I was going through the "initiation" part of the ascension journey.

What exactly is a Psychic? What makes them so different than everyone else? And how did they get that way? A psychic is someone who has tapped into the universal knowledge bank, and can access it whenever they want or need. That is the only difference between them and the average person. Psychic abilities come in many different forms such as: seeing ghosts or spirits, seeing them and communicating with them, healing others by touch, predicting the future, knowing what is wrong with someone medically, etc.

So how did psychics become psychics? They raised their vibration to the point where they were able to access a realm of knowledge not accessible to people who have not done so. Some of them were born that way, they have always had access to it. Others, like me, worked hard to reach that level of enlightenment. Each one of us, however, has the ability to reach that place, and develop our own unique gifts. The only question is: Are you willing to do the work necessary to get there?

Your personal vibration can be measured by the types of thoughts you have on a regular basis. The lower you are on the spectrum, the lower your vibration. Basically, people living in high vibration have released all the trauma, drama, shame and blame that many of us carry around like a set of luggage. We show off this luggage by declaring how hard our life is, how everything is always happening to us, repeating "Look how hard I have it...." At every possible opportunity and to everyone who will listen.

As long as you are living in the victim stage of life, you are not able to access love, happiness, joy and enlightenment. The reason for this is that pity, sadness, jealousy, fear, anger, and pride are like anchors. They will keep you at the bottom of the ocean, unable to rise to the surface and breathe fresh air. They are all encompassing. They do not leave space for you to access everything that requires weightlessness.

My first bit of advice about this whole process is that you find yourself mentors: People who you trust that have already gone through this process, and who can support you. These people will be necessary along the path. Going it alone, although not impossible, is like most things in life not the best or easiest way of doing it. Science can now measure the frequency of thoughts, and lower frequencies are all those thoughts that fall below 200 on the scale below.

The process of ascension involves consciously raising your personal vibration and thought frequencies so that you gain control of, and start to affect, your life and experiences. At 500, or LOVE, you gain the abilities to manifest and draw to you those experiences, people and synchronicities that change your life. In short, what you need to know is that once you start living from love, things start to happen. In order to activate your intuition and access your higher knowledge, you must release those things that block them. This is done by releasing negative beliefs and emotions which keep one stuck in the daily victim mindset.

As long as you are in victim mode, you will not have access to your intuition. Most of the people on the planet are not optimizing their true potential. They have accepted the belief that life is hard, that everything happens to them, that they have no control over their experience.

Below is a chart from David Hawkins's book *Power vs. Force* (1995) of the vibration level of a person, which he calls "Log", and the correlating emotional experience. David Hawkins studied energetic frequencies of people and Using techniques derived from kinesiology, Doctor David Hawkins presented a method by which one can gauge consciousness on a scale of 1 to 1000, where 1 is simply being alive and 1000 is the ultimate state of enlightenment. As you can see, he documented the full continuum of the human emotional range.

Enlightenment	700
Peace	600
Joy	540
Love	500
Reason	400
Acceptance	350
Neutrality	250
Courage	200
Pride	175
Anger	150
Covetousness	125
Fear	100
Grief	75
Apathy	50
Guilt	30
Shame	20

(Hawkins, 1995)

Rev. Michael Beckwith, a spiritual teacher who founded the Agape Church, summarizes the levels of energetic growth into 4 distinct stages. While these stages do follow a progression, they are not linear. This means that you can flow between them. Achieving stage 4 does not mean that you cannot go back to 3, 2, or 1. It just means that in 1 area you have managed to rise to the highest levels of vibration. Although these stages are fluid, you must progress through them in order. You must master stage 1 before you can move to 2, and stage 2 before moving to 3 etc. The fluidity happens between the stages you have already mastered, and those before them. The 4 stages are as follows:

> *Stage 1 - "TO US." The victim stage. Life is doing something to us. On the scale above this would fall roughly between 1 - 199*

> *Stage 2 – "TO IT, BY US." The manifester stage . We are doing something to "it." We are making something happen with our mind. On the scale above this would fall roughly between 200-350*

> *Stage 3 – "THROUGH US." The Channel. We are yielding. We are allowing. We are open. We are letting. On the scale above this would fall roughly between 351 - 599*

> *Stage 4 – "AS US." The Being stage. We have become aware that our life, and the life of god, and the life of joy, and the life of life itself is our very own life. On the scale above this would fall roughly 600 and above*

(Beckwith, 2008)

According to Beckwith, you have to master stage 1, the victim stage, by finding the filter you are using to interpret the events of the life you have been living and releasing it, then 2 by visualizing the life you would like to live, then 3 by allowing that life to show up and trusting that it will show up perfectly, then 4 by finally allowing the divine knowledge to become a manifested through you. Once you reach stage 4, you are no longer resisting the universal order. You are living in a state of complete flow, which allows you to access your intuition fully and act on in without doubt.

Many times throughout my own journey I would have loved to grab a book that gave me more than lists of symptoms that people may go through, but actually explained how those symptoms showed up for a real person. This book covers what I actually went through. These are not the only ways the symptoms can show up, but according to conversations I had with others who also went through this process, some of which will be discussed below, they were fairly common across the board. The shift from left-brain linear thinking to right-brain intuitive knowing is a very large shift, but well worth the effort, if you can make it through.

Prior to starting this journey I thought I knew who I was. I was determined, tenacious, and always doing something to make my life better. I had a good set of friends and never really felt lost. In the past two years, as I went through this process, I felt like my life had flipped upside down. I was constantly exhausted and felt so alone all the time. I didn't know what my life meant anymore. This journey will force you to look at your existence as a whole, and make you question everything about yourself and your life. I felt like I had lost myself and had no idea who I was or what I had done with myself until now.

One afternoon at Starbucks I was talking to a friend named Danielle who was also going on this same journey, but was just a bit behind me experience wise. We were discussing some of the things we had gone through and were going through still. During our conversation she complained about her pants not fitting as well the past few weeks. She said that she didn't understand what was happening, because she was eating well and exercising regularly. There did not seem to be a good reason for it. I mentioned the "Buddha Belly" effect. She'd never heard of this. I told her that since I felt as if I was going through this alone I had done exhaustive research about the ascension process and what happens.

I was practically a walking encyclopedia on the symptoms commonly referenced by those who have compiled lists of effects they have encountered. I have included these lists of symptoms at the end of this book. I found them so confusing, and contradictory. She looked at me with a funny expression and told me that she was afraid to do any research because there were so many viewpoints, she couldn't know who to believe. Aside from that, the only two categories of information were 1) Lists of symptoms which were not very helpful, and 2) The wonderfully happy "How wonderful life is now that you are a psychic" books written by those who had already finished the hard part of this journey.

We complained about the many articles out there sharing the same long lists of symptoms, and videos talking about what may happen all wrapped up in 5 minutes or less. The problem was that all of these were pointing to the end of the process, created by people who had already gone through this and were talking vaguely about something they had experienced in the past. There was no help, no support, no one saying XYZ were totally normal and, further, here was how they showed up for a real person. No one taking us through the process as it unfolded. No way for us to reference and check in with the severity or lack thereof of something we were going through *now*. Just lists and anecdotes about the promised world that awaits us. Even then, they did not tell us what we were headed toward specifically.

Were we going to be channels, psychics, empaths, healers, all of the above? What does the end actually look like, and how do we know when we've arrived? Did each psychic ability have its own set of symptoms, and if so could our symptoms hold the clue for where we would end up? I will answer the last question now. NO. The symptoms are not indicative of where you will end up. Each of us has certain abilities at our disposal. The symptoms do not relate to a specific gift. The symptoms are what happen as you are releasing the lower vibration from your energy field, and raising your vibration. That is why they are fairly common across the board.

So here I am, writing the book that I wish were at the store for me to pick up and read as I went through this. Although I will talk about my personal experiences, I have talked to many people who have also gone through this and I've found that most of what I've felt and experienced is common. It just hasn't been documented. Just know that if you find yourself thinking "I am the only one going through it, so that makes me weird or crazy." You are not. When you think "I must be the only one going through all my challenges, right?" You are not.

The Beginning of the Journey

For me, this journey started many years ago. Throughout this process I felt lost, scared, confused, exhausted, a bit excited, and incredibly apprehensive about the whole thing. You need to know there are only two options through this Journey: 1) Go through this experience and receive it exactly as it comes, accepting responsibility for handling the consequences, or 2) Declare that you are not interested in ascension and ask your guides to stop the process. Decide that you want to stay as you are and live the rest of your life without this change. For me, the latter was not an option. Now that I knew there was a whole other set of options and possibilities to explore, I was *all in*. I will tell you that if you choose the first option like I did, that choice will be tested regularly and at times severely.

Having completed the grueling first part and coming out alive and well on the other side, I can tell you this: It was one thing to think I wanted "to Ascend", it was quite another to actually go through it. It was hard, it was messy, it felt bad (even horrible) a lot of the time, and I had to ask myself up front, and many times throughout, "Am I willing to go through with it no matter what happens?" The answer to that question was what I needed to hold on to when the going got tough, and it did.

I had to keep reminding myself that I asked for this, and stand firm in my decision. There were times when I questioned whether it was worth it. I'm not telling you this to scare you. I'm telling you because it's something that everyone goes through, many times. You truly need to have the strength to keep reminding yourself that you chose this, and you are all in. Or, ask for it to stop and let it go away. Just make sure, whichever choice you make, it is what you really want, because once (if) you decide to stop, it is most likely a final decision. Your soul will obey whatever command you give it.

You don't get to decide when you're ready. Trust me, I tried. If there was a way, I would have found it, and no one could have kept me out of the club. I was all ego, stubbornness, driven desire, and left-brain linear thinking. I thought that if I chose to do this it just happens, starts, sucks a bit then is over. Boy was I wrong. No matter how good you think you are, or how badly you want it, or how much you think you deserve it, it is not your choice. Spirit, God, the Universe or your Higher Self (whichever term you want to use) has a path which must be taken and rules that need to be followed, and there's no loophole that will speed up the process for you. The term is not really important as some people believe in God while others see a universal source, while others still believe it is their own higher knowing. For the sake of this book I will use the term Universe to refer to this higher intelligence.

You can't force it, beg it, speed it up, or convince someone else to let you in the club. Once you come to grips with that, and accept that you need to relinquish control, you may be allowed to audition your way into the club, and if you pass the audition, possibly be allowed to begin learning how to play the game. The "audition" is the series of challenges that come up as you shift to a higher vibration. Frankly, most of the process is an audition because at any point, you can choose to walk off the stage and say "I quit."

You will not know when the audition starts, what it looks like, or how long it will take. Going to a psychic and paying them to make you psychic, and asking them to open all your chakras and connection to source will not work. I tried that, with a wonderful psychic named Estella. We are now friends, and I seek her guidance regularly. She has become one of my most trusted mentors.

I went and did all the chakra openings (unblocking the energy moving through your chakras), and energetic clearings (removing stale and unwanted energy from your personal field, sometimes called the aura). I felt the process, I saw the visions, I experienced the openings, these things are different for everyone, as you will see later in the book. Each person receives information in a different way, so where I can see visions (they come in the form of a movie which I watch until I have all the information), some people may just know something, others may feel it physical.

There is no right or wrong, it is all about getting to know who information comes to you so that you can use it. What she told me was that I had been opened up, but until I was ready, nothing would arrive. That was completely accurate, but not what I wanted to hear. It was also something that I could not fully grasp until I had gone through it. The "being ready" does not mean that you decided you wanted to do it. It involves your brain and physical chemistry rewiring to be able to access the higher levels of information which need to communicate with you. The only thing you have control over is whether you declare your willingness to begin the journey or not. Beyond that, everything is out of your hands. It is up to the Universe, and your body.

I truly hope that this recounting of my personal journey, and the lessons I learned from it, will be helpful for you along your journey. Although my journey started several years ago, it did not truly take off until 2014, when I was in a complete melt down on my couch, staring at my favorite Buddha picture, in the fetal position, hugging pillows (because there was no human around to hold) and crying my eyes out to the Universe about my life and how badly it was going, saying "I surrender. I have nothing left. I can't fight any more. This is too hard. If you have a plan, help me, please!" Emotional meltdowns are normal especially at the beginning of the journey. I liken this to boot camp. You have to be torn down in order for all the things that do not align with you to release. Only then can the new information and way of being come into your reality.

This happens when you begin questioning everything you think you know. The entire way you have been living your life. All your beliefs, all your thoughts, all your judgements. This does not mean that you throw out everything you have ever believed. What it does mean is that your truth will come in to question, and you will become very clear on what resonates with you and what doesn't. The things that don't will go away easily and naturally.

As part of the lower frequency release, you will also start letting go of things that happened in other lifetimes. This will bring up fear, anxiety and a deep sadness that seems to come from nowhere. This is very close to, if not actual depression. When these emotions arise, don't try to stop them, Allow them to release and move out. They are blocks that have been trapped inside of you for a long time and need to be removed. They are very natural.

Several years ago, shortly before my move to Dallas, I started doing past life regressions with a psychic friend as a trade for some Feng Shui work I did for her. A past life regression is an experience where you go into a meditative state and are guided to see yourself in one of your past lives. She was taking me through past life experiences where I had created energetic blocks. Energetic blocks occur when you experience something that is traumatic and too hard to deal with. Your emotions become too intense for your body or mind to process, so they create a wall. Think of these like brick walls that take up space in your body.

They are very real and do actually take up physical space in your body. They can cause diseases and other physical problems. Many people report that when they release a block, they suddenly feel as if there is an emptiness in part of their body. As if something has been removed. This energetic wall gets buried in your energetic body as a safety mechanism. The idea is that it is buried and not available to be dealt with. Clearly it was so bad that you could not deal with it the first time, so as a protection mechanism you locked it away.

The problem with these blocks is that they prevent you from evolving. You will continue to repeat some form of the original pattern that led to the block over and over again. This is your soul trying to point you to the area which needs to be cleared in order for you to grow. The only way to get past the pattern is to find the block and deal with it by releasing the issue once and for all. Many people think that in order to release a block you need to re-live the trauma. This is not correct. There are many instances when simply recognizing that there is a block and allowing the block to release itself is perfectly ok. You do not always have to know what it is, where it came from, who caused it, what it did to your life, etc. It can just release on its own. The way I work with blocks is asking my higher self to release the blocks in the easiest and least traumatic manner. I state that if I need to see it in order to release it, then that is what should happen. If not, I would like it to clear without all the drama.

I found a very effective technique for dealing with those blocks which you need to see and relive in order to release,. What you can do with these is go in and re-write the story. You go through the original trauma once by watching it unfold as you remember. It does not matter if what you remember is what actually happened. Your interpretation of the situation is what matters, because that is what created the block. Once you have gone through the whole memory, go back and change it to how you would have liked it to happen.

I heard someone who had been ridiculed by his principal at school when he was a child change the story so that he stood up to the principal. He told the man exactly what he thought of him. He turned the story around so that he could be the hero. When he was a child he could not do that, so now as an adult he stepped in and stood up for his younger self. I was told that at this point "It is very important to specify that this does NOT mean altering your actual memories, i.e. denying reality in favor of a delusion you like better." (Shamay, 2016) But that is exactly what this means. It means actually going in and rewriting your history to something that is not traumatic.

There is nothing wrong with removing traumatic memories from your mind's databases and replacing them with good ones. The idea is that every cell in your body is a kind of memory storage. Every time you think of a traumatic event, you are rewriting that story into your cells. By doing this you are keeping the trauma alive forever. Your mind is the software which runs your life. When you have a defective code on your computer which causes programs to crash repeatedly, you would not think twice about replacing that code with one which produces the desired results. So too here, you are replacing defective code with something that produces the desired results.

When I did this with one of my most traumatic memories, it was gone, or rather the charge that it had for and on me was gone. It was as if it had never happened. Now when I try to recall it I have a very hard time doing so. I do remember that there was a memory there, and what that memory used to be. What I can't do is access it as a memory. What happens when I try to recall it is that it feels like trying to bring up a dream that is fading. It is lost in a fog that I have to strain to see through.

Back to my past life regressions. In my sessions we had gone through at least 10 past lives that I could remember. We never spoke about what my friend was seeing from her end, and it never occurred to me to ask for her insights as I assumed that the sessions were about my experiences and what I was going through. I assumed she would tell me if she saw something important that I should know. On the same note, she never offered her own insights, keeping them to herself.

This was a very important introduction for me to the art of healing others. A true healer / psychic / channel does not NEED to talk about any messages they get. They do not have to pass on the messages at all. They can choose to pass on the messages if it is appropriate, and they usually know if that is the case. Either way, they should never translate the information they get. It is important to pass on the information exactly as you get it. I will talk more about this later.

One day, about a year after my last regression, during a conversation with her, she told me that I was an incredibly powerful psychic. She had done many past life regressions with people, and had rarely seen anyone accomplish the kind of energetic clearing and releasing that I was able to make. I had managed to remove things from my auric field which had been trapped there for a very long time. It was unusual to see so much clearing and shifting which could affect the present life of a person by altering the past. She had never said anything to me about this because she didn't want to scare me. Little did she know that instead of being scared, I was exhilarated.

I finally had an explanation for what I had experienced in my life!! Many things made sense all of a sudden, like why I attracted people who needed healing. I did not know at the time that this was my particular gift. I found that out later. I also seemed to experience a lot of paranormal activity that others did not. I had always been a huge fan of magic shows and super power shows, and used to wish that I could be that kid. The one who goes their whole life being normal then finds out they could do magic, or some other fun thing that made them unique. Well, turns out I was that kid. I just never had anyone to guide me along the path.

But, now what? So I was a really powerful psychic, or at least had the potential. But what did that mean? What could I do? Where was the instruction manual? Where was Dumbledore to instruct me, Harry Potter, about the cool world to which I had been introduced? Nowhere in sight, that's where. No Dumbledore, No McGonagall, no Snape, No one. Apparently I had the powers buried deep inside me but had to find them alone.

It turns out that this is very common. There are very few people who are born into families where generations upon generations have nurtured their gifts. Many generations hid their gifts, but if you listen closely you may find that others in your family also had them. One of my relatives spoke about meeting angels when he was young. I heard stories about another relative cursing someone who had defrauded them. This was not an evil sorcerer kind of curse. It was the asking for karma to hit the person who had hurt them. A very important point to make here is that while high vibration leads you to enlightenment it is separate from having psychic powers.

There are people who are born with these gifts that choose to do bad things. What you will come to see is that the higher you get on the vibration spectrum, the farther away you get from doing bad things. Enlightenment and peace are closely connected. Some people hear stories about their grandmother curing people who were sick just by using herbs, or with thoughts. The problem is that these gift were hidden out of fear, and not taught and nurtured in the generations that came after them.

For some reason, after this initial conversation, I was drawn to Reiki. Reiki is one of the many methodologies used in the holistic healing arts. It falls under the healing touch umbrella, along with Trinity, Arching light and other modalities. Energy healing is a way of working with the electro-magnetic fields, or aura that surrounds a person. By working with these fields, one can cause physical, spiritual and emotional healing. Apparently, Reiki is the gateway methodology for many people into the world of healing energy. Most uninitiated healers start with Reiki, then branch out toward other methodologies or practices. I was drawn to it very intensely, and also to a specific master. A Reiki Master is someone who teaches others how to work with Reiki energy. This master echoed the sentiment that I was very powerful, so the confirmation was there.

During these classes I started connecting with my angels, guides, and guardians. Although I try not to say these are universal beings, they are experienced in the same way by everyone I have met. They are also similar to the religious mythology of these beings. The fact that most religions have some version of these beings, tells me that they are experienced by everyone in the same way. These are entities which surround us and are there to help us throughout our lives. You know what angels are.

What you may not know is that each of us has one primary angel that stays with us our entire lives. Their job is to protect us and make sure we are ok. You may know them as your guardian angel. Aside from your guardian angel, you have many other angels who come and go depending on your needs at the time. In addition to the angels, we have guides. These are entities which may either have lived and passed on then come back to help, or they may have never incarnated as humans, and are devoted to helping us live better lives.

While going through the Reiki classes I asked my teacher what my next step should be. How do I get clients and start working on people with my new skills? She told me that once she was attuned, she just put the intention out to the Universe and customers started showing up. Putting the intention out to the Universe means that you are clear in your thoughts and are not distracted by negativity. You believe that it will happen and trust in that fact. So I did the same. I decided I was ready and asked the Universe to send me clients. Nothing. Crickets. No one even remotely close to coming into view. No one interested in letting me work on them.

It wasn't until later that I was able to understand why this happened. I was sent a Youtube video explaining what happens energetically. This video discusses the fact that just because you can do something does not mean you are ready for it. You will attract customers that mirror where you are in your journey. If you are a huge mess, you will attract people who are huge messes. This could lead to a really bad dynamic and make you miserable. You will grow to hate what you wanted to do. Worse yet, you may pass on bad energy to others as you work on them. To avoid this, the Universe will prevent you from having this experience, and inflicting it onto others. You will simply be blocked from finding customers to prevent such consequences.

You should note that there are many teachers out there who use different media for their message. Some videos are just as good, if not better than, face to face learning. What matters is what will resonate for you, and how you best receive information. Some will capture you immediately, others will make you cringe, and still others will not be your cup of tea but will have gems of information that you can use. Give everyone a chance, and see how their information sits with you. There is nothing wrong with not resonating with someone, or some method of learning. That just means that person, or method is not your teacher, and that is perfectly ok.

To be completely honest about the situation, up until recently I had been a major drama queen about this whole process. I wanted it, I wanted it now, and I was not happy with anything less. I would get very annoyed anytime my mentors told me I had to wait, and they couldn't give me what I was asking for. I became jealous anytime I heard that someone else was getting what I wanted. I was constantly comparing myself and my abilities to those of everyone around me. Such impatience is a common experience, the way it is when learning any new craft. This experience was also echoed by my fellow students when we had private discussions, so I knew I was not alone.

Given how much I was comparing myself to the progress of others, and my unwillingness to allow the process to unfold as it should, it was no wonder that I was not getting clients. It would not have served either of us for me to put that energy into someone else. This is the same as being negative around someone. They will feel it and react. The difference is that when you are working on someone energetically, they are open to what you are doing and very susceptible to your energy. They may pick something up without knowing. I was simply not ready.

So I had wonderful skills but no way to attract my clientele. I really wanted to be able to make a wonderful living helping people. I think this is a very big challenge that I encountered along the way, and believe that it deserves special note. I know many healers who down play their gifts and minimize the importance of charging money for their work. Many healers and psychics think that you should not charge because it is not spiritual. Many people who go to these healers and psychics feel the same.

I don't believe that my gifts, or those of anyone else, should be free to the world any more than an architect's or lawyer's gifts should be free. If you are providing a service, you have every right to expect to get paid for that service. "When you give up your resources to provide for someone else's needs, it is only fair to expect that they will reciprocate and help provide for yours in turn. You believe that it is more important to spend your energy healing those who need healing rather than making a living for yourself some other way. It is only right that those who accept your healing help you make up the loss you've accepted for their needs, in this case a monetary loss." (Shamay, 2016)

I believe that it is just as important to be a receiver as it is to be a giver. Many people think that since the gifts are spiritual in nature, they should be given to the world freely. Those same people never question that many religious institutions make money happily in exchange for their spiritual gifts. There is nothing wrong with combining spirituality and finances. Every time there is balance to maintain, exchanges must be equal on both sides, and in this physical 3D world the energy transfers through money or a trade of services.

For example, I am happy to not get paid cash for a session if I get an hour long massage, or something of equal value. That is a fair exchange of energy, but at the end of the day our rent needs to get paid just like a lawyer's rent, and in this reality that happens with cash. All this is not to say that you can't ever do something nice for someone just because you feel like it. That is not at all what I am saying. It is, however, important that you be comfortable getting paid, and more importantly asking for payment, should you decide to use your gifts in a business capacity.

The process of learning Reiki or any other methodology requires a lot of change in your life. You will go through a cleansing process. This could be a spiritual cleansing, it could mean your relationships turn upside down, it could mean job changes, it could mean physical changes. The clearing process is different for each person since each person has their own areas that need to be improved. What is common for everyone is that as your vibration rises and you connect more fully with your higher self, you will go through clearing. There is no getting around it.

Becoming a Reiki Master / Teacher means that I had mastered the use of Reiki energy and was able to pass that energy along to others as a teacher myself. Once I attained Reiki Master / Teacher, my master told me that my life would turn upside down. Everything that was not in alignment with who I was becoming would disappear. Once you embark on this journey, you start finding your true self. This is the person you were meant to be before family, society and friends told you that you should not be that way, or that your dreams were too big, or whatever version you happened to come across.

Somewhere along the line, you may have stuffed your true self down in a hole so that you would not have to deal with disappointments, or explanations about who you are and how your life should really be. Holy cow, was she right. My left brain linear thinking led me to "YES!!! My dream life was coming!!!!" Well, not quite. My life did turn upside down. But what I was not expecting was getting stuck hanging upside down, with everything falling out of my pockets and no way to grab on to anything to help turn myself right side up.

I was not expecting the work I would have to do to be given a handhold in order to flip myself right side up. This again is normal. Things and people disappear from your life, very quickly at times. All of a sudden, things you used to like no longer interest you. You find that you start questioning everything you thought you knew. You lose the desire to do things you used to love and see people you were once close to. You may go into a sort of hibernation where you feel lost and alone.

What I did know was that nothing in my life up to that point had worked right. Not just in the way that it was not happening the way I had planned, but that nothing I seemed to do was successful. I tried job after job hoping that circumstances would be different. It was always a massive hunt for a job. Then it was getting a job which paid the bills, but that I was not in love with, and finally moving on because it wasn't right.

It seemed that no matter where I went, nothing changed. It was always the same scenario. If only I had known then that my soul was trying to get me as far as possible from the life I had been programmed into thinking was correct. My soul was trying to send me into the life I was supposed to be living. I have seen with many people that nothing will work out well for you until you are on the right path. You will be forced to redirect yourself over and over until you start moving in the right direction, until you are in alignment with who you really are. Some people do this quickly, and others take longer to learn that lesson. I was the latter.

How do you know when you're on the right path? Life starts to flow easily, and you stop hitting walls. It is easier than you could imagine to get there. Any pursuit that makes you feel happy, that brings you fulfillment, that keeps you from being unwell is leading you down the right path. Anything that makes you unhappy, sad, depressed, angry is not. When you stop doing anything and everything that does not feel good or make you happy, you will shift your life effortlessly. This does not mean stop doing everything and sit around meditating all day. If you have bills to pay that would not be a good idea. Getting to your goals takes work, sometimes a lot of it. What it does mean is that whatever you do will feel effortless. When you are doing the right things, you will be able to do them all day, and it will not feel like work. A great example for me is this book. I can easily sit down in the morning and start working on it, and not realize 5 hours have passed.

I decided to get rid of everyone in my life that did not make me feel supported. All the people who I had tolerated and just kept around because they gave me something to do, even though when I was with them I was not happy, had to go. Any loving, supportive relationship should always make you feel good about yourself. You should always feel cared for and safe with whomever is in your life. I also stopped doing any activity that did not make me happy or feel fun. I decided that there was nothing wrong with only being obligated to me. The fact that someone wanted me to do something, or thought that I should be somewhere, was not reason enough for me to do it. I now only commit myself to those things that will make me happy.

Until you get to the point where you are in alignment, nothing you try will work properly. Once you've found the right direction, however, things will start falling into place without any effort at all. Assistance that you never would have dreamed possible will arrive just as it is needed, sometimes before you know it is needed, and doors which you never saw in front of you will open.

This is the magic of finding your true purpose, the reason you are here. The Universe truly does all the hard work for you. Granted you still need to do something, you can't just sit on the couch watching TV and expect everything to fall in your lap, but what you do will feel easy. Everything becomes easy, and help falls in your lap, sometimes before you know you need it, when you take the right kind of action. The right people start showing up. You find yourself in the right place at the right time. Whatever you need appears.

You need to become comfortable with allowing and receiving. You must allow energy to flow even when something happens which seems like a disappointment. An example of this is how I found my dream office. I had been looking for an office location for a while. My gut told me it would be in a particular area, but I ended up looking in other parts of town because the person who was helping me thought other areas were better. Estella my psychic mentor had just found a new space and was moving in. The day before her move I was having coffee with Danielle, and we were talking about Danielle helping Estella move in to her new office the next day.

Danielle invited me to come help and hang out with them. The challenge was that the following day I had a lunch appointment that had been scheduled long before. I was very much looking forward to this lunch because it was a possible business opportunity. The second factor was that Estella herself had not invited me to come help, and I assumed that she and Danielle may be doing some energetic work together along with moving into her new office. I told Danielle that if Estella reached out, and the lunch appointment canceled, I would come.

Monday morning, moving day, arrived and I got a text from Estella inviting me to meet them at her new office around 10. Completely unrelated to my coffee with Danielle, as they had not spoken about the invitation that had been extended the day before. I explained that I had another appointment, but if she canceled I would definitely come. 30 minutes later my lunch appointment cancelled. I went to meet my two friends, and as we were setting up her new office Estella asked if I wanted to take a tour of the building. I was happy to, as it was a very nice location, so we walked down to the leasing office and asked the leasing rep to show us around.

She started showing us the empty offices in the building. The second office she took us into was perfect. I saw the suite and knew it was my new location. It also happened to be in the part of town where I had initially thought to look. My gut had been right, and the right set of circumstances had aligned to let it all happen. My ability to allow the situation to unfold as it did, without stress, created the right environment for manifestation.

Another example of allowing and receiving happened last Halloween. My friend Erica and I had been considering joining an invitation only travel club. The proposition Seemed like a great deal, and we would get amazing discounts on all our travel. Halloween night around 9:00 PM as Erica and I were celebrating at her house, I got a call from the person who handles the memberships for this club. He told us that his boss had agreed to an incentive for that night since he wanted to close out the month strong. Half off the membership fees plus a couple extra bonuses. Erica and I discuss it and decide that we would join right then and there.

When I gave the guy my credit card, though, it didn't go through. We tried twice without success. I called the credit card company to find out what was going on, and was told that my account had been frozen due to fraud. They would not give me a new number and would not unfreeze anything that night and I had to wait for my new card. I did not have a debit card with me, so I could not do the transaction, and by the time I got home it would be too late. There was no way for me to get the special.

I was very disappointed, and honestly really upset by this whole thing. Here was this amazing deal, with major discounts, for something that I really wanted. How could this be? Why would the great and powerful Universe prevent me from getting this great thing? I later found out that it was one of the greatest gifts I could have gotten that night. When Erica went to the website to make use of her membership, she found that all the promises were not backed up by reality. She could not find any packages that she wanted, and when comparing their costs with those of a regular travel agent or travel site the deals were not good at all. 6 months after joining she decided to cut her losses and terminate the membership. What I had seen as a major disappointment and let down, was actually the Universe taking really good care of me. Sometimes being in the flow means not getting your way. Many times you later find that the huge annoyance was really an amazing gift.

It was important for me to not look at unexpected events and disappointments as bad, regardless of how much I wanted something to happen. Once I was on the right path, there was a very good reason for what seemed like setbacks at the time. When I let myself be open to all the unexpected circumstances that arose, I was able to see and receive the wonderful rewards that arrive. It may take a while for you to see the benefits of unexpected changes in direction, but they are always there. Have faith.

Personal Connections, Your Tribe, and Everyone Else

One of the less obvious, but harder to deal with symptoms of going through the ascension process is the change in your social circle. This happens to everyone at different times, but it happens none the less. As your vibration rises, it will be hard to maintain connection to people who are not on the same path. This will manifest in many ways, but the common theme will be the ending of relationships which you thought were very important to you. This will not always be by choice, or even conscious, it will just happen. Sometimes the other person will leave you. This does not make either of you a bad person. What it means is that you have shifted to a place where they are no longer comfortable following, and they choose to grow in a different direction from the one you are heading down. That is OK. It also means the beginning of other relationships, ones that reach deeper than you thought possible before.

Fairly early in the process I started noticing I had very few people in my life that I could talk to about the ascension process and symptoms. The problem wasn't finding people; over time, I had managed to cultivate a group of great people who all understand this journey. The problem was that between work, their kids, and life, we never seemed to be able to connect. That left me with my old friends, whom I love dearly, but didn't or couldn't understand what I was going through. No matter how much I tried to explain what I was going through to them, they just could not relate.

The people who tried to understand did so from their own experiences. Without some frame of reference, people reach for the information and contexts available to them to try to make sense of new information. 100% of the time, the people available to reach out to were unhelpful, not because they didn't want to help, but because they had no perspective or reference point for this kind of shift and how it affects the body, mind, spirit and emotions.

One of my friends kept telling me that it must be my thyroid. Clearly the fact that I had no energy, wanted to sleep all the time, had an appetite that seemed to be all over the place, had mood swings and bad days must be symptoms of a thyroid problem. She had personal experience with thyroid problems and a good frame of reference for them, and she imposed what was wrong with her on to me. I have also heard people tell their friends that they are depressed and should be on mood stabilizers, that they are crazy, that they are drama queens, etc. My friend even offered to pay for my blood tests so that I could see for myself what she already "knew". It didn't matter that I had already had a very thorough blood screen done, which showed I was very healthy.

She was unable to accept that she was wrong. My experiences didn't fall in line with her experiences, and she could not comprehend, let alone accept that her explanations were not the right ones. This is something we have all done at one time or another. Someone comes to us in distress, and out of desire to help, we search through our memory banks to help find a solution. My old connections couldn't support me through the process. I was left alone to figure this out.

When you find yourself in this place, know that although you may feel alone you really aren't. There are many times throughout this journey, and the rest of your life afterward that your soul will isolate you from the world. This is needed, so that you find yourself and your own answers without the influence of others. This is the only way that you will eventually be able to stand in your own knowledge, power, and truth. You will come out with clarity, confidence and certainly about your intuition and what is right for you that you never had before.

I also found that I was having a hard time both connecting with, and maintaining connections to anyone who had not experienced this process. I felt as though I was going through all the motions of being a friend, and maintaining contact with my old friends, but the deep feeling of connection was gone, severed. This applied to my friends, my family, everyone who was not directly part of my new Spiritual Tribe. I did not mean to drift apart from my old friends. It simply happened, whether I liked it or not, and it left me very isolated and lonely.

I experienced a deep down, painful kind of ache and longing for a heart level soul connection with other humans. I know I was always surrounded by Angels and Guides and Spirit, but I ached for human connection. I knew other people were not feeling this disconnection from me because any time I sent out a message saying I felt alone, I got many, many responses showing me how many friends I had. The problem was that I did not feel connected to any one of them. This does not last forever. Eventually you will connect back with your friends, if you choose to do so.

Your spiritual tribe will emerge as you grow. These will be your friends, your mentors, those people with whom you connect and who will be able to support you and later be supported by you along the journey. These people will either be going through the process alongside (at the same time as) you, or be your mentors, or be those you will mentor.

I had no desire to go out to meet new people. I had no desire to be near people at all most days. While I sometimes thought that it was not healthy to spend so much time at home alone, the thought of going out, being around strangers, and making conversation seemed painful. My intuition and empathy was expanding so quickly that being around people also made me feel sick at times. I was now able to feel other people's emotions, which was overwhelming. This could happen with anyone, not just people I knew. There were times where for no reason while talking to someone I would have to hold back tears. There would not be a rational explanation for why I would be so sad, but it would happen. It is overwhelming because you are bombarded with everything that everyone is carrying.

We are not built to feel the whole world's emotions. Very often we have trouble with just handling our own. When you become overloaded with feelings and thoughts that do not belong to you, you can become ill. One day I had gone to a Botanical Garden near my home and found a nice secluded spot near a waterfall. I was very relaxed listening to the water, which was keeping all other noises at bay, and there were no people walking around so I felt at peace.

The little corner I found was off the walking path so no one came near me. I finally decided it was time to start walking back using the trail that went behind the waterfall into the grotto. I sat down inside for a while to enjoy the sound of water. Shortly after I sat down, several groups of school children came through in succession, some stopping to enjoy the space and sounds. After about 5 minutes I felt so physically ill and emotionally in pain that I had to leave. Not just that spot, but the gardens altogether. I felt as if I was having a panic attack along with the stomach turning that happens when you are about to pass out, and the body aches associated with the flu all at once. This lasted the whole drive home. All I could think was "I need to get home. Home is safe. Don't stop. Home is safe" Indeed home was safe. As soon as I walked in the door I felt better.

You may start to notice that your home starts feeling like more of a sanctuary than it ever did before. This is because your personal belongings absorb your personal frequency. My home was filled with my energy, my personal frequency. Since mine had gotten so high, it was hard being away from that vibration level for too long. You will also start to notice that the general vibration level of the world around you is much lower than your own. This will be uncomfortable at times. It may make you feel disconnected, irritable, sick, or just ambivalent in general. A very good question to ask if you are not feeling well, or your mood changes suddenly is "Does this belong to me?" This question causes your energy field to check around and find any foreign energy that has attached to you.

The only times I seemed to be at peace was when I was in nature. One day I was walking toward some grass, and felt as if I was connected to it in the same way I want to connect with people. How could I connect with grass, you might wonder? All I can say is that it felt like I was in the company of an old friend. I could relax and simply *be*, and didn't have to make any effort to get the energetic filling that I needed. At that moment I did not feel alone or isolated. One afternoon I decided that I needed to go to the lake, and it had to happen *right then*. I got in my car and started driving. When I arrived at the lake I instantly felt better. I sat down at the base of a tree and felt all my pain and stress disappear. I felt as if everything was ok, and I had all the support I needed. It was there, in nature that I started to really feel the presence of my guides and angels. I felt like I was not so alone, and that things would work out.

Your guides and angels are always around you. The challenge that we all face is that we can't hear, see and feel them all the time. Find a place where you can go retreat, a place where you can be calm and quiet. Somewhere that makes all the noise in your head stop. This is where you start to hear your guidance. It comes in quietly at first, and almost seems like your imagination making things up. Don't be fooled. That is how your guides communicate with you. Subtly and quietly.

Prior to starting this journey, I never realized how low the general frequency of everyone around me was, and how many people were hurting, angry or unhappy. We all know that in general many people are not happy with their jobs, or relationships, or health etc. Understanding that most people are not happy on an intellectual level doesn't come close to the experience of feeling it inside of you, and being overwhelmed by it coming from every direction at once. I never realized how far our aura, or the electro-magnetic fields that surround our bodies reach, and how it impacts others. You will start to feel how being around certain people affects you. I started researching how to raise my personal vibration so that I would not be affected by everyone else's, I also looked into what the effects of raising my personal vibration would be on me and those around me.

In general, people don't really think about how their thoughts affect their bodies. In great part, our lives tend to run on automatic tracks that are pre-set for us. We go to school, where we are taught how to get a job working for someone else. We get a job, where we sit in whatever environment happened to come with the job. We settle into a routine life, where we wake up, go to a job we don't necessarily like, possibly working with people we don't like who also don't like their jobs, leave work, maybe go have a drink with some friends, go home, go to sleep, then wake up and do it all over again.

The ramifications of this kind of life are severe, but are rarely talked about, maybe because very few people fully understand them. When people have a job that they dislike, or work around people they dislike, it affects their thought patterns. Many times, those thought patterns become toxic. You long for your two days off, probably Saturday and Sunday, but those days are usually cut short because by the middle of Sunday your brain starts thinking about the following day and how much you dread it.

In school we are taught that our bodies are around 70% to 80% water, but very few people understand what that means for their health. In the eastern philosophy of health, it is explained that we create our own reality. That our thoughts affect the world we experience. The world we live in is simply a projection of our internal thoughts. We do not see what we experience, we experience what we see, think, and feel.

If you see the world as a happy helpful place, that is what you will experience. If you see the world as a scary, mean place that is what you will experience. This also affects our physical body. Our thoughts are energy which is absorbed by every cell of our bodies, and stored there as a memory until we release them.

Dr. Masaru Emoto was a Japanese author, researcher and entrepreneur, who claimed that human consciousness has an effect on the molecular structure of water. He experimented with water and demonstrated this very thing through photographing crystals. He exposed water to everything from Heavy Metal music, to different thoughts. His experiments showed that water was very much affected by the energies that were projected on to it.

You can find more information about this in **Messages from Water 1** (1999), **Messages from Water 2** (2002), **Messages from Water 3** (2004), and **Messages from Water 4** (2008)

It was 1994 when the idea to freeze water and observe it with microscope came upon me. With this method, I was convinced that I should be able to see something like snow crystals. After two months of trial and error, this idea bore fruit. The beautifully shining hexagonal crystals were created from the invisible world. My staff at the laboratory and I were absorbed in it and began to do many researches. At first, we strenuously observed crystals of tap water, river water, and lake water. From the tap water we could not get any beautiful crystals. We could not get any beautiful ones from rivers and lakes near big cities, either. However, from the water from rivers and lakes where water is kept pristine from development, we could observe beautiful crystals with each one having its own uniqueness. The observation was done in various ways:

Observe the crystal of frozen water after showing letters
to water
Showing pictures to water
Playing music to water
Praying to water

**Taken from
http://www.masaru-emoto.net/english/water-crystal.html.
(Emoto, 2010)

Given how water is affected by external thoughts, imagine how our bodies are also affected by the energy that comes in. If you were constantly thinking unhappy thoughts, the water will become contaminated with bad energy. This will cause health failures. For me, the final parting with this kind of life was after a year where I became severely sick every six weeks. Right on schedule I would come down with some bug that landed me in bed for seven days, barely able to make it to the bathroom or couch, let alone the kitchen to make food.

At that time I had a job that paid very well. I also had a horrible boss who would openly call me stupid at the top of her voice in the middle of the office. I was asked to do the work of five people in a forty hour work week with no overtime. No one wanted to listen when I told them their request was impossible. I had to create my own system to keep things going the best I could, then was reprimanded for not using a nonexistent system they wanted which would have taken 4 times as long.

I would go to bed arguing and yelling in my mind, and wake up with the same arguments filling my head. When I would pass by a window at work, I would look out and think "FREEDOM." I remember thinking that I would rather be unemployed and broke than having to keep going to this job which made me miserable. I was also listening to a lot of hard rock music at that time. It seemed to be the only thing I could relate to. It was also the only thing that would relax me. No

42

wonder I was constantly getting sick. All the energy that was flowing into my cells, bombarding me in my daily life, was toxic.

Just as a frame of reference, when I am in good shape I listen to meditation music, classical, some Celtic. Today the thought of putting on anything loud and hard makes my body recoil. To me it sounds angry, and as demonstrated by the water crystals not really healthy for our bodies.

Personal Boundaries and Holding Your Own

Something else that had started happening was the personal boundary challenges from both humans and spirits. There had been several nights when I felt a psychic attack while asleep. Psychic attacks are when lower vibrational beings try to get into your energy field to cause damage. The occurrences that happen while sleeping are different than dreams. They are very clear and make perfect sense both in the dream state, and afterward. There is no interpretation needed. It is as if you are actually living the scenario in a lucid state. This is different than a lucid dream. In a lucid dream you know you are dreaming and start manipulating the dream to create fantastic events. During these attacks you are an active participant, but not manipulating the situation, you are actually participating as you would while awake.

During The first experience I was fully aware that there was a threat coming toward me and that I needed to defend myself. It was much more powerful than a dream in that I was controlling the situation, but not aware that I was in a dream state. The second night this happened, I was in bed in my dream, but it felt as if I were lying in bed awake. My sheets started to flap around me as if a powerful wind was blowing them up. Then my bed began to rise and fall. After several minutes of this, someone behind me began to poke / push me in the shoulder with a finger. It was so hard that I felt it bruising me. I didn't know who it was and couldn't turn around to see them. I was, however, aware that I was in my bed, and that I was being attacked by someone who did not belong there. I had started waking up and was coming out of the dream, but the poking was still happening.

I managed to stop them by declaring that they were not welcome and must leave. They just laughed as if it was some kind of joke. I then demanded to know who they were, and images started flying through my mind. The images finally stopped on the cat I had when I was a child. It was clear to me that this being was not my cat, and I rejected that thought. I again banished this creature, this time for good. Several seconds later I was fully conscious, but rather than being alarmed or upset, I was calm and relaxed. It took me a minute to get my bearing and realize I was in my room in bed. I was fully aware that it had been a psychic attack within a dream. I can't explain how I knew, it was just true. I also knew that I had mastered some kind of lesson, as I was able to defend myself while unconscious.

You will find that as you go through this kind of work and process, some knowledge will just be. You will know things without being able to explain how you know them. There will be an internal compass that turns on and tells you certain things, and you will not have to question that knowing. It will be very clear that what you know is true. This is normal. It is you tapping into your higher self. The most important part of this experience was that I was able to defend myself during this interaction at the unconscious level. It was at this moment that I understood, and completely accepted my arrival in my own power at the unconscious level. I realized that my higher self was protecting me at all times, and that I had nothing to fear.

I had another night time (dream state) occurrence that was similar. I was looking at what appeared to be a wall, then the wall changed into a sort of veil. I saw faces and arms trying to reach through to me. These were good beings, not ones that wanted to harm me. I knew they were good because I was not afraid. I did not feel the need to defend myself against them. It was like seeing old friends who wanted to say hello. I was happy to be near them and that they were trying to reach me.

I acknowledged them and was excited that they were trying to connect. I was happy to see that the separation between the material world I was living in, and the energy world where other beings exist was thinning for me. The dream continued and I moved into an empty, dark space. It was here that I felt a very large and powerful energy coming toward me. It was as if I had sensed a nuclear bomb go off somewhere in the distance, and was waiting for the shockwave to come my way. I had no idea what this energy was, or what its purpose was, but I was not comfortable with its eminent arrival. Seconds before it hit me I managed to call angels and had them surround me. I felt the energy hit and woke up. I was a bit confused and was not sure if I had summoned help in time, but I knew I had asked for help, and tried to believe that it had arrived. The impressive part, and the one that made me feel safe, was that I was taking care of myself at the unconscious level.

Personal boundaries were also being challenged on the corporeal front with my non-psychic friends. I was noticing that my friends had started to react in ways that I was not used to or prepared for, and when confronted, they also had no idea where these reactions had come from. One friend had started to criticize me publicly in the form of mean and aggressive verbal attacks. This happened a couple times, and I quietly dealt with it. The third time was very loud, very public, and very nasty. I had asked a couple friends I know, who were going through this ascension process, if they were also experiencing this phenomenon.

They both said that they were experiencing it as well. It seemed the personal attacks from friends were escalating in severity to the point where we had to question whether we want these people, these "friends," in our lives. People who had been there for long periods of time, and with whom we were close, at least until that point. These attacks happen because the difference between our vibrational level and that of those friends causes them to start shifting vibrationally as well. For many people who are not ready this shift is very uncomfortable, and they will lash out at a subconscious level.

What they are telling you is they are not ready to shift, and are trying unconsciously to stay exactly where they are. The most common outcome in that situation is a parting of ways. You will start to feel uncomfortable around them, and they in turn will feel just as uncomfortable around you. Eventually something will happen to sever the relationship so that you can continue on your path of growth and they will be able to stay within their comfort zone.

The interesting thing was that while these attacks were growing in severity, I had noticed that my ability to deal with them was also growing. Prior to this process, I would have just ignored it in an attempt to maintain peace. I would have assumed that something I did brought it on, as it must be my fault that this happened. Now not only was I not tolerating these situations, I was standing my ground and making it clear that this behavior would not be tolerated. I was also managing to deal with it in a very calm, rational manner. I was clear about the fact that although I will not tolerate this behavior they were still my friends, if they were willing to respect me and my boundaries, and I was coming from a place of partnership. I wanted to find a way to make the relationship work, as long as my needs and I were being respected. Since we were friends, I wanted to work on the situation as partners, rather than adversaries, to find a solution. Giving them the opportunity to maintain the relationship if they wanted.

Physical, Emotional and Spiritual Symptoms

Don't fight the pain, allow it to flow. I want to start this chapter off with a bit of counter-intuitive advice, particular to this process, which was a life saver once I discovered it. A lot of the emotional challenges that you will experience along this journey are due to energetic junk coming up for release. This junk needs to release, to let up the pressure, and if it is coming up that means that you are ready to let it go. All of it will feel bad. It may come in many forms from anger to sadness to depression, but it will definitely come. What I found was that if I just acknowledged it, allowed myself to feel it, and allowed whatever was surfacing to flow it would pass quickly. It would definitely come on more intensely, like a hurricane, but then it would end just as quickly. I would not be struggling for a long time. I have heard many people talk about how depressed they feel for weeks or months, or they just feel horrible for no reason. This is because they are trying to fight, or suppress the negative emotions hoping to not feel them.

There were several times where as I was driving and had to pull my car over to the side of the road and just cry my eyes out for no reason. Not just a little cry, but a full bawling breakdown that I could not control. This was usually accompanied by feelings of being trapped in my life situation, having nowhere to go and no options for moving forward. If I tried to fight it I would experience this feeling for hours or days. If I stopped what I was doing and allowed myself to feel the pain, I would bawl my eyes out for 5 – 10 minutes, then the whole thing was over. All of a sudden it would be like the blue skies that appear after a huge storm. I was able to be happy once again, and the world returned to being a wonderful place.

All through this journey I have been very healthy, at least according to any western MD that could have been asked. I want to note that because as you read about the symptoms that come up you may ask yourself "Why didn't she just go to a doctor." I am addressing that now to get it out of the way. I had a full checkup done, full blood panels, full physical, full everything before I started this journey, and again recently. Both western and eastern practitioners ruled me HEALTHY. What I did do every time a symptom came up is go to Estella and ask her. Without fail, each and every time she had a number of stories for people going through the same thing. I also asked other people I know who were on this journey at the same time, they also reported the same symptoms. Conclusion, this was not illness, it was spiritual clearing which needed to happen. To this day, I am one of the healthiest people you will ever meet.

As your personal vibration rises, and your energetic field starts to clear, you will start experiencing physical manifestations of this clearing. Your outside environment will start to reflect your inner world. This is because our reality is a projection of our internal situation. Your eating habits will change, sometimes randomly and for various lengths of time. When the physical manifestations started to occur, it took me a little by surprise. My body first decided that the vegan eating habits I had cultivated over years, and which my body had always appreciated, had to go out the window as one day I was overwhelmed be a meat eater's cravings.

My body insisted that for 2 weeks straight I would eat nothing but tuna salad (super heavy on the mayo and onions) and chocolate. I could eat as much of those two things as I wanted, but nothing else. At first I was only allowed to eat after 4 PM. When I say allowed, I mean that any divergence from these rules, like trying to eat at noon, resulted in immediate and violent sickness. I was physically not able to alter the plan which my body had created out of nowhere. After a week I could start eating at 2 pm, then a few days later noon, then a few days after that at 10 am. Even with the time variation, I could eat nothing but tuna salad and chocolate.

The unique part of this was that I had essentially been a raw vegan for five years by that point. It was a system that helped me function well, and which I did not have to force because my body was happy with that way of eating. For my body to take a 180 degree turn like this was interesting, to say the least. This pattern recurred once more about 6 months later. The second time it was beef instead of tuna, but still the same phenomenon. I had also stopped dreaming, and was not sleeping well at night. When this happens it is because your body is using a lot of energy as it goes through huge changes. Your cravings will change based on what nutrients your body needs at that particular time.

This eating change did end about 3 weeks after it started when one day I woke up and just wanted my vegetables back. I had stopped wanting any animal products at all. The smell, taste and thought of eating them was not appealing. I wanted nothing more than a huge salad and fruit. I was so excited that I ran right out and bought lots of them. It seemed that a reset had been accomplished and I was now over the hump. You will know when a shift is occurring because all of a sudden a random change happens. For me, the smell and taste of the animal based food was not appealing after wanting nothing else.

Your physical environment will also go through a transformation as your vibration rises. I live in a 2 bedroom apartment, and was nowhere near a pack-rat. I did not think that I owned a lot of unnecessary things. I would never have come close to being portrayed on the TV show Hoarders, and was rather tidy. One day I had the overwhelming urge to start clearing my apartment. I had belongings that just had to go. They were actually annoying me so badly that it was physically painful to have them in my space.

I started with the kitchen, clearing out all the cabinets. I brought out a ladder so I could reach all the high shelves, and remove everything that was a problem. This was not along the lines of something that could be done casually while taking my time. It was a burning desire to remove, remove, remove. I emptied out my cabinets and left only the bare minimum. Half of my shoes were either donated or trashed, whether they were good or not. Many decorations were removed from the walls. This continued for about a week, each day emptying another room. By the end I had either thrown out or donated seven or eight large trash bags of things.

Looking around my apartment, it felt empty, but in a good way. All of a sudden I could breathe in a way that I had not been able to do for a long time. This process lasted for a couple months, but not at such a massive and speedy rate as it had in the beginning. Every so often, I would open a door or drawer and find something in there that needed to be thrown out. Sometimes the whole cabinet or drawer needed to be handled right then, regardless of what other plans I had. Just when I thought I didn't have anything else to get rid of, something else caught my attention.

I asked Estella if this had ever happened to her. She started to laugh and told me that her house is pretty much empty. Not the kind of empty you or I would imagine, but no furniture, no drapes, nothing empty. She said one day she just needed to get rid of everything, and she did. If you encounter this phenomenon, it is completely normal. What is happening is that your vibration has changed so much that everything in your environment that does not align with you has to go.

The physical signs showing you how your energetic field is being cleared are quite unmistakable. One day I decided to change out a light bulb in a torch lamp in my living room. I had used this lamp for a long time, and it did not light the room as well as it should. The new bulb flooded the room with light, just as I had remembered it should. I had known that the old bulb was past its prime, but did not realize how much until the new flood of light hit. The problem was that after 5 minutes, the lamp shut off. Apparently the old wiring was able to sustain the new intensity for a short time, but then had to shut down. I took that as a physical sign of my outer reality reflecting my inner one. The old vessel could no longer sustain the energy which was flowing in, and needed to be changed. Likewise, the change that happens to our body is a physical upgrade. Without that upgrade we would not be able to handle the amount of "light" that starts flowing through us as our vibration rises.

One of the themes in the whole ascension journey is paying attention to the signs that arrive. These could be physical signs, emotional or "gut feeling" signs, or thoughts that seem to come out of no where. One morning, about 6 months after my ascension journey had started, I walked into my living room to find that one of the nose pieces on my glasses had been uncurled and was sticking straight up in the air, and the glasses themselves were twisted. This was another and very clear physical manifestation. This had happened over night without anyone being near or touching them. My personal energy was affecting things around me.

Up until this point, I had been complaining that I did not have a road map for this process, and it was hard to just let go and trust that I was heading in the right direction. From everything I was experiencing, it seemed the Universe was listening, and agreeing. You will find that your guides, angels and the Universe at large have a rather interesting sense of humor. As I was driving somewhere one afternoon, I got a little turned around. I plugged in my GPS to find that the entire memory card had been wiped clear. The physical signs were all over the place, mimicking what I was experiencing. The trouble was, I still had no idea what was going on inside me, and what it meant. If I went by the physical signs:

1) I had released most of who I was as a person up until that point. Throwing out much of what I had held on to without a second though.

2) I was now fairly empty and need to be, because nothing new could come in as long as I had so much old baggage taking up space in my world. Again, throwing out everything that did not suit me.

3) I upgraded to a higher energetic vibration and my old body was not able to handle it for long periods of time so needed to be physically changed in order to handle the higher frequency of vibration. Lamps were not working, remote controls were malfunctioning.

4) All my old navigational methods and routes were no longer of use and new ones needed to be installed. They would be, very shortly. And they would not look like anything I was expecting. This meant that the way I had been living, and navigating, my life until that point was no longer applicable. I had to find a new way to get where I was going.

5) Since no one was there to tell me where to go, I would have to figure this out myself and trust that the rollercoaster I was on would get me to my destination. This part was not true, I had mentors all around me, I just had not yet seen them for who and what they were.

The physical and emotional sides, up until now, seemed to be mimicking the spiritual. As I was doing all the spiritual work, releasing all that stands between me and the

Universe, I was constantly tired. There were days I woke up tired and didn't get better. Some days I woke up excited about life and happy, then crashed by noon or one o'clock. From there it was just pushing through until bed time. I was not sleeping well or at all some nights, and I had stopped dreaming completely.

Many days I would feel depressed or, at best, neutral, and there was a very great sadness that I couldn't get out from under. I could find nothing to feel passionate about. Then there were the breaks. Those days when I woke up full of energy and happy, excited, calm and relaxed, when I remembered what life was supposed to be like. It was basically a hodgepodge of energy and emotions. When the many lists of ascension symptoms I had found on the internet say you may feel crazy, they mean it. I was not sure whether I was manic depressive, purely unhappy, needed medicating or just going through the nasty mess and needed to hang on because it would end soon.

These emotional ups and downs are very real, and need to be acknowledged. As you go through this process, you will be releasing many life times of sadness, sorrow, anger, etc. Sometimes the feelings are very hard to deal with. That is completely natural and normal. There is nothing wrong with you. Mine were hard to handle, not so severe that I was incapacitated, but some people do get to the point where they feel incapacitated. If you find yourself overwhelmed or feeling suicidal it is VERY IMPORTANT that you seek help. Speak with your mentors or find someone you trust to help you through this.

Do not try to go through emotions that severe alone, because you are not alone. If you start feeling suicidal, please find someone to speak to. For some people it is definitely part of this process, but it is one that you should never try to go through alone. Pay close attention to your thoughts and feelings, and get help immediately if you find yourself thinking of ending your life. You will get through it, because it is only temporary, no matter how hard it feels in that moment.

I had started learning the difference between actual physical sickness and the symptoms associated with processing energy. Energetic processing comes and goes depending on what shifts were happening. Sometimes it felt like sickness, but did not have all the physical symptoms that come with an actual illness. I had also learned that I could ask for help from my guides in processing and integrating the energy which was coming through my body. When I did this, the symptoms tended to lessen or go away completely.

You can ask your guides and angels to schedule such processing for times when it will not affect your life, like during sleep. Their job is to make your life easier, These beings are not ruled by ego. They do not do this in order to get anything out of it. It is a job they accepted because it serves the greater good of moving everything closer to enlightenment. So you should feel free to ask for whatever you want or need. There are no limits on these requests, so be creative and have fun with the process. The only limits are your own blocks. If your beliefs are in the way of what you can manifest, then your requests can not be granted. As long as you are living without resistance to what you are asking for, you will see it appear.

The Exhaustion was almost unbearable some days. It was as close to narcolepsy as you could get without actually having the disease. Some days I woke up full of energy and life, excited about the day. I saw all the possibilities and how great everything is. Even those days were a challenge. Most of the time, somewhere between noon and 2 PM I was hit with exhaustion which was so strong it was a battle just making it to the couch. I was so tired that I couldn't think. Falling asleep once there was the only option. If I decided to push through it I had to make a very strong caffeinated drink, double caffeinated, and drink several just to get me to bed time.

Until the exhaustion phase I had not been a user of caffeine, and knew that when I did need it usually a small amount would suffice, but that was no longer the case. It would then take an hour or so to get my brain moving. This in no way meant I had the energy to go anywhere or do anything. I could work a bit, or do other things that required very little thought, but not much more. Other days I woke up tired, as if I had not slept for days, and my energy level dropped from there.

The Buddha Belly was another fun one. I had started losing weight, and was very excited about that until all of a sudden my pants started getting tight. At first I was worried that I was reversing my weight loss, but that soon turned out to be a non-issue. My body was doing two completely opposing things. My legs below the knees, and my upper body above my waist seemed to be shrinking. I was wearing shirts that had not fit in quite a while, and the calves on my pants were getting more and more loose. Everything between my knees and belly, however, seemed constantly distended. God forbid I ate any sugar, because I swelled up like a balloon and pants that had managed to be comfortable in the morning seemed to shrink around me. This is a common phenomenon. Everyone I know has gone through it at one point or another.

The Buddha Belly started happening shortly after my tuna salad experience. As soon as I went back to regular food, I swelled up like the Michelin man. I also started waking up with puffy eyes, and some days a puffy face. I started suffering from night time allergies. This was not normal for me as I had always been healthy without strange bags or swelling around my face. I decided it was time to see an expert, so I made an appointment with my acupuncturist.

He checked me out and told me that my problem was my spleen. I was taking in way too much sugar and had to cut back most of what I was eating. This came as a shock because aside from the tuna salad & chocolate situation I was essentially a vegan. Nothing but fruits and veggies. As a rule, I don't crave sugar like the average person. I didn't eat starches, no gluten, very few legumes. The only sugar in my life, for the most part, was fruit. So now my body was becoming hyper sensitive to any and all sugars, and that meant fruit needed to be cut way down. The sensitivity was bad enough that a whole pear would make me swell up. Some days the fruit was worth it because I really wanted a treat, but for the most part, I was now super limited on food choices.

I was also hypersensitive to chemicals. The plug-in scents I had in my apartment had become overpowering and I could smell the chemicals behind them. I could smell the underlying chemicals in almost everything. Perfumes which never bothered me, now reeked and gave me headaches. My skin also became very sensitive. There were very few things I could use to wash my body. I had to change out my soaps and shampoos until I found something that did not produce an allergic reaction.

These reactions could take any form, and happen anywhere on my body. My most common variety manifested as an eczema like outbreak on my hair line. Any time I used a soap or hair product that didn't work it appeared within minutes. Anytime I ate something I shouldn't, it appeared.

Basically I had to watch everything that came my direction, and had a very immediate and visible reaction to show me what didn't work.

Hot flashes were another new symptom. I would wake up in the middle of the night radiating heat. It felt like a full body fever. My skin was very hot to the touch, and I could not cool down. These were not menopausal hot flashes, nor was there sweating. This was truly the feeling of my body turning into a furnace and burning up from the inside in an attempt to cleanse unwanted energies. It was almost impossible to cool down when this happened. I remember making a body cooling spray of water, lavender and peppermint.

Peppermint on the skin has a cooling effect. Most times it feels as if you are getting cold. Even this spray would not work when I heated up. The second way the heat manifested was a warmth around my hands, feet, face and other extremities during the day. This was much less severe, and felt as though there was a cloud of heat surrounding whatever part of me was being activated. It felt like someone had pointed a heater at that particular part of my body, and I was surrounded in a cloud of warm air. It would then migrate to other parts of my body, legs, feet, torso, chest. There were times when I would look for cold metal to touch just to remove some of the heat.

I was affecting electric items like phones, cars, radios. There was a particular day when a friend invited me to go on a boat ride at a local lake. I was drawn to a particular part of the boat near the back, and just wanted to lie there all day in the sun. The boat was rather large and there were many place which would have been much better, and much farther away from the engine exhaust, but for some reason I did not want to leave that particular spot. I was there a few good hours relaxing in peace. When it was time to go, we all congregated inside and the captain tried to start the boat. After a couple failed attempts a couple people walked to the engine to see what was going on.

Turned out that the engine was directly below where I had been all day. It seemed that I had drained the power out of the battery. They did not know that, but they did comment on the fact that this had never happened before. That explained why I had been feeling so good and relaxed all day, and why I had not wanted to be anywhere else on the boat. I was replenishing my energy from the battery. I realize that this sounds impossible, but it happens and is a normal symptom when your vibration changes and starts interacting with the energies around it. This is just like draining a phone battery faster than normal, or your car battery dying regularly even though it never happens when other people drive that car.

Other strange electric phenomena were happening as well. My cell phone battery was being drained at an alarming speed, and when I would take it in to have it looked at by the techs, I was told there was nothing wrong with it. My car's electric system was malfunctioning on a regular basis. My home stereo's remote control refused to work. I was unable to hold my cell phone anywhere near my body as I was having a conversation with people. Anytime I put it into a pocket so I could work while talking, the call would disconnect or the connection would get severe static interference.

I had always been a user of the corded hands free, but now it became a necessity as I was not able to keep the phone on me as I spoke. I was living in an apartment at the time, and two nights in a row as I was having the severe hot flashes the fire alarms went off in my apartment and the apartments directly connected to mine. Only those apartments connected to me were affected both times.

The inner shaking that people talk about is a little more difficult to explain. I used to have hypoglycemia. The first few times the shaking happened, it felt like that. When your blood sugar drops too low and you get that internal shaking. Another way to describe it is like being plugged in. Sort of like having yourself plugged into a socket which is sending off a much stronger current than you can hold, so you fell the extra electricity zapping you constantly. I used to call it "The shakes." The shaking associated with a vibration change feels a lot like that.

When it was a larger frequency jump, I also felt the queasy stomach and light head that comes when you feel like you are going to pass out. It comes on strong, lasts a while, and when your body has fully assimilated the energy it goes away completely.

Body aches and pain are yet another set of symptoms. As you process energy, and increase frequency, your body has to release toxins in order to be clean and hold a higher vibration. It also has to reconfigure the internal structure of your organs and bones to handle the higher frequencies. This will cause pain.

Some days I felt like I had worked out way too much the previous day and were now suffering from severe lactic acid build up. Other times the pain would gradually grow. Starting from my lower back one day, the next adding my mid-back, and then my upper back and neck. Like my muscles were being overused, or underused and complaining. It would last a while, then I would wake up pain free, as if it had never happened.

The most severe days felt like I was 90 years old, and everything hurt no matter what I did. Physical pain was not limited to muscles and joints. I also had days where my skin hurt. It was so bad that a breeze touching my skin would cause pain. It was like my nerves had been rubbed raw and there was no way to cover them. The only thing I can compare the skin pain to is a few times when I had a high fever. During those times, it hurt for anyone or anything to touch me as if my body had become hyper-sensitive. This is the same feeling. It can last an hour or a few days, and during this time there is nothing to do but deal with it.

My sense of smell became incredibly heightened. Some people may think this would be wonderful, because you can smell all the flowers, and nature. I can tell you that from my experience this is not amazingly wonderful. What I was smelling was everything around me. Until this point I had not realized how much poor hygiene there is out there. Many people smell. They just do. I could smell mold and mildew. My car and apartment would smell incredibly musty if I did not leave the windows open to air them out. I will point out that I am really clean. It would be one thing if I were messy and did not clean often, then it would make sense that my car would smell bad, but I take my car in for a wash every 2 weeks at the most.

This was a whole new awareness of all the smells around me. Anyone who wore perfume or cologne smelled as if they had showered in it, regardless of how much they had actually put on. Being around smokers or people who had been drinking was just horrible. Not only did the alcohol and smoke smell, but also the people themselves. This is just a cautionary warning, so that when you start noticing symptoms like these and decide to not frequent certain places you used to love to go, keep in mind that this is just another symptom of this unique journey.

Another very interesting symptom which I was experiencing was breathing trouble. When I shift frequencies and begin processing a new level of energy, the old energy that needs to leave comes up for release. At these times I had noticed that my lungs seem to close. It felt as if the top third of my lungs closed and became inaccessible. Normally when I take a deep breath, the air feels like it starts filling the diaphragm and center of my lungs then works its way up all the way to the top. When shifts happened it was as if the top third of my lungs was closed and the air simply could not get up there. I was not able to take a full, deep breath. I would have to stop, adjust my body and force the air to move in. Sometimes it worked and sometimes it did not. I didn't feel like I was suffocating, but it did feel uncomfortable.

Are you Psychic Yet?

Comparison is usually your downfall. One of the easiest ways to miss out on the wonderful gifts which you are developing is to compare yourself to others. As long as you are focused on what others have, and how great what they can do is, you will miss the beautiful gifts which you are receiving, worse yet, you will waste valuable time which you could have used learning how to use your gifts and refining them on coveting something that someone else has. Just as each of us has different physical traits such as green eyes, blue eyes, blonde hair or brunette hair, so do each of us have unique abilities. Some people can see spirits and talk to them, others can heal with their hands, yet others can see medical problems within people's bodies. No gift is less important than any other. No gift is ever wrong. You were given your specific gifts because that is your strength. Enjoy it, relish it, learn it and use it. No one person can do everything.

For a long time I really wanted to see ghosts and spirits and talk to them. I hoped and prayed for that ability to show up. Alas, that was not mine to have. One day as I was lying in bed I thought about how lucky I actually was for not having that gift. I can go to bed and know that I will get a full night's sleep without some random spirit waking me up just because they need to talk right then. I really, really love to sleep. I can give up a lot of things, but that is one that I would not appreciate losing. I don't have random entities following me into the bathroom needing to chat. I have quiet because there are not random entities popping in and out at all times. Sometimes, what you think of as a loss is actually an amazing thing.

For a while I had been able to see the energy around electric street lights, plants, power lines. I could see it by relaxing my mind and looking at the negative space around objects. Negative space is what most people consider air. Anything that is not a solid object. What I saw specifically was the object itself surrounded by what looks like a gray cloud. Some days the cloud was bigger, some days smaller. It seemed that the energy was not a perfect match for the object, meaning that it did not always surround it in a perfect outline. It gets bigger in some areas, then tightens up in others. This energy also leaves a trail. So when I am driving, the gray cloud surrounding a tree will linger a bit as the tree was getting closer. It seems to blend into the air around it.

This is different than the after image left when staring at something too long. If I am just sitting watching the branches of a tree move, the cloud will move with the branches. It will not stay in one place as the branch moves like an after image would. I noticed that the more relaxed I got, the more prevalent the energy's visibility. The air had started becoming less clear. As if I could see layers blending into each other at times. It was kind of like looking through water, or static, but it was clear. Kind of like looking through very old windows, where you see the silhouette on the other side, but the window is not completely transparent.

I started making contact with energy beings while awake. These are different than guides. Your guides are like your energetic support system, there to help you. Think of them like your friends and family here. These other energy beings would be like the rest of the world. Around, but not really your team. I had felt a presence near me in the 24 hours prior to the first event. The hairs on my arms started to stand straight up, and when I asked if anyone was there my body tingled. It was a very wide spread tingling, and covered a large area of my body, as if it were responding to my question. The sensations happened at random times, but were always accompanied by the feeling that someone I couldn't see was near me. Several times as I was walking and feeling scared or upset I called certain angels. I could feel a very large, very solid being for lack of a better word walking along side me. As if there protecting me.

The second type of contact happened while meditating. I was sitting comfortably, and very relaxed one afternoon. I was in that twilight state where you are almost asleep, but still conscious. I felt someone squeeze my calf. It was not hard, or painful, but it was definite contact. It felt as if someone had wrapped a large hand around my calf and squeezed gently. Just enough to make themselves known, and get my attention. While it did surprise me, it was not scary. I retracted my leg and woke up fully. I asked who it was and told them that I was open to communication if they felt like connecting. Silence. Not a hint of who or what it was.

Channeling is an interesting experience. Many times as I am working on people energetically, I will get messages. Usually it sounds like someone is talking to me. I will hear specific words or whole sentences. Sometimes I will even see someone or something in the room. The images vary and can take on many shapes. Often what I see comes in the form of a movie. It will keep playing until I have gotten the message, then end.

Guides, Entities and Energetic Boundaries

Who are guides and what is their role? A guide is a being who has chosen to hold an active support role in your life (assuming you allow them to). They have taken on the responsibility of advising and steering you. They may be someone you knew who has passed away, or they may be beings who have never incarnated here. There are also different types and levels of guides and different vibrations as well. There are high vibration guides whose energy is positive and uplifting. Their advice will always feel good, and calming. Guides are available to advise you on any issue that can arise, but will not force ideas on you. They will give you pointers and possibly lead you in the right direction, but they will never give absolute answers. Everyone has access to their guides, but not everyone is aware of it. Many people are completely oblivious to the fact that there is a whole support system out there for them just waiting to be used. One does not need to be on this journey to interact with them. What I have found is that most people not on this journey are simply not aware of their existence.

What you get from them is possibilities, all of which are right, and none of which will cause you problems or bad feelings. These guides can come in many shapes and forms, and can send messages in many ways. The guides will also change throughout your life depending on your personal circumstances. I have a guide who is a cow. Yes, the kind of cow you would find on a farm. I have several guides who look like people. I have some who I have never seen. Danielle has the spirit of a child she knew who passed away when she was young. Estella has her grandmother and other family members around her. In healing sessions I have seen some people who have fairies as their guides. I have also seen dogs and cats. They may plant a thought in your head, or come in a dream, or have someone say the right thing to you at the right time. Their messages are subtle, and gentle. Never pushy.

Your guides, angels, and other high vibration spirit helpers will never step in and try to take over or cross boundaries. They will wait patiently until you ask them for help, at which point they will spring into action. Their advice will always be gentle and feel good. It will leave the decision up to you. A high vibration guide will never take the decision and choice away from you, as they are there to assist with your soul mission. This is one of the easiest ways to identify which type of "assistance" you are dealing with. High vibration guides will also try to help a few times, and then stop if you ignore them. Think of them like everyone else in your life. They are more than happy and willing to help, but will not waste their efforts on someone who does not want the advice. Don't worry, when you finally decide that you want them, they will be there for you.

Once I fully understood who and what guides are, I had a conversation with my guides. I acknowledged that I may not always hear what they are saying. I explained that it is very possible that I am just not getting the message, even though I have been told many times, and they think I have already heard. I asked them to keep sending me the messages, and assume that if I am not acting on it I have not heard them. I told them that if I get a message, and want to ignore it, I will tell them directly that I am choosing to not follow that piece of guidance. This seemed to work well, because after that conversation I started getting much more clear and solid guidance. I was also getting the information in multiple ways and multiple times. They did not give up on me, assuming that I don't want their advice.

I have one guide who kept showing up in readings. A cow. Yes, the farm animal. At first I was upset that I was getting a cow. I could not see how this was a good sign and just assumed a random spirit came to play. She would not say anything, just stood there and looked at me. I told her to leave twice, rather annoyed that I was getting some ridiculous farm animal. I wanted to get a tiger, or a dragon, or some other powerful beast to come aid me along my path. The third time this happened, as she was leaving (because I had told her to go yet again) she left me a red diamond. Not physically, it was part of the energy that was in the vision. These gifts are not part of an energetic commerce system, more like a friend giving you a flower. They are just presents to show that you are valued, and appreciated.

The following day we had an open house at my office, and one of the ladies was telling me about her grandson. She looked at me as she pulled out her phone and said "I don't usually do this, but I just feel like your life will not be complete unless I show you these pictures of my grandson at Halloween." It was him in his costume for Halloween. He was dressed as a COW. Point taken, guides, point taken. I decided to look up what the cow represents as a spirit animal. Imagine my surprise when I saw "Spirit of the great mother goddess... Isis connection.... Nurturing... Femininity" etc.

I will never turn that guide away again. My ego had rejected something incredibly powerful because it did not come in the "right form." Many times when dealing with the energetic world things will not come in the "right form." They will not arrive all neat and clean and pretty like you would expect. Many times, the biggest gifts will show up in the least expected packages. You may be having a bad day, and feel like everything is going wrong, and no matter what way you turn, the opposite of what you expect happens. More than likely, what you will see later on is that things were going exactly the way they needed to in order to help you out the most.

The reason you felt like everything was going wrong, was because you had an expectation of how it should be. You had a plan, and that plan was perfect (at least in your mind). The problem with your plan is that most of the time, your plan will not lead you where you ultimately want to go by the fastest, shortest route. Your plan is flawed. You just can't see it. Here is where you go back to trusting that things are lining up for you regardless of how it looks in the moment.

There are also low vibration guides. These are beings who's energy is angry, unhappy, desperate, causes feelings of scarcity and basically make you feel bad. These guides are not usually the ones who will give good advice. When you hear from them the answers will come from a place of scarcity, fear or anger. They will be happy to take over your life and give advice on what you need to do, or how you have to act. This guidance will never feel gentle or good. It will cause you to feel bad, and act accordingly.

When you get advice that feels pushy, bad, or abusive, this is a clear sign that you are not being advised by high vibration guides. Not all those who come to advise and help you have your best interest at heart. Sometimes, they may not be bad beings, but they are not high vibration and therefore will not serve you in a good way. There are spirits and guides who retained their personalities after leaving the physical plane. They may or may not know what is in your best interest. As an example: If your mother was not the person to go to for advice while she was alive, she is probably not the person to go to for advice now that she has passed. There is nothing wrong with interacting with her, but don't forget who she was when she was here, and take her advice with a grain of salt.

There are also those who do not have your best interest in mind at all. They can give "advice" which could be detrimental. These are low vibration beings who are not invested in happiness, harmony, and helping you further your personal journey. They are the ones who will tell you what to do, and be relentless about it. If you ask them which decision to make, they will always jump in with an answer and make it seem as if you don't have a choice. It will feel like if you don't do what is being suggested your life will fall apart. Be very wary of this kind of help, just like you would with a living human who did the same. I know that when you feel lost or afraid it feels great to hand over the reins to someone else and tell them to make it better. That is not the role of your divine assistance.   Their role is to guide you, but ultimately leave the decision to you. They will offer options and possible solutions, but these will never come with a doom and gloom feeling attached. And they will never give you absolute answers because you have free will.

It is always a good idea to ask for help from only the highest vibrational guides available to help. This removes any being who will not serve your highest good. If you were trying to learn a sport, you wouldn't ask just anyone for help, you would ask for help from that sport's MVP's. That is essentially what you are doing by asking for high vibration guides. The two do not go through a power struggle vying for your attention. Since your intention is what determines what happens, simply ask for only high vibration guides to show up and they will.

I know someone who specifically asks for the help of the highest vibrational beings available at that time. No matter how you phrase it, just keep the intention that you only want help from these beings and you will be ok. You can also just set a permanent request that you only receive help from the highest vibration guides going forward. Remember that with energy you can ask for anything, there are no rules or limitations. The only limitations are your own beliefs. When I first realized this, I asked that I only deal with the highest vibration guides forever. I also put certain guides on permanent assignment to help me be happy and get amazing gifts every day. Again, there are no rules, so you can ask for whatever you want.

When you are feeling scared, or low or angry try asking "does this feeling belong to me?" This question speaks to the energy that you are in at the moment. That question alone changes your energetic vibration, and allows your body to actually stop and examine what is happening. It also helps to add "If not, I demand that you leave." This will clear your energy, and remove any external baggage that you have picked up. This works with headaches, muscle aches, poor moods, basically anything that does not feel amazing. Once you have tapped into the world of energy, it is very easy to start picking up things that do not belong to you. I find it very helpful to clear my energy on a daily basis. Energy will accumulate around you, sort of like dust. If you do not clear it off regularly, you find yourself in a pile of dirt which starts weighing you down.

The world of energy responds to clear instructions so it is very important to be clear and firm. One of the most bizarre premises of quantum theory, which has long fascinated philosophers and physicists alike, states that by the very act of watching, the observer affects the observed reality. Scientists have now demonstrated that light particles will act differently depending on who is observing them. If someone thinks the particle will travel in a straight line, it does. If the next person thinks it will bounce around the room, it will. In a study reported in the February 26 issue of Nature (Vol. 391, pp. 871-874), researchers at the Weizmann Institute of Science have now conducted a highly controlled experiment demonstrating how a beam of electrons is affected by the act of being observed. The experiment revealed that the greater the amount of "watching," the greater the observer's influence on what actually takes place. (Science, 1998)

This shows that we are directly affecting our realities. Because of this you must set very clear boundaries and believe that they will be obeyed. The energy world listens and respects boundaries, because they have no other choice, and it will not disobey once you have made yourself clear as long as you are firm in your conviction. The reason it will not disobey is because disobedience is a contradictory behavior. Energy always responds to your requests with a "YES." Anytime you feel like the Universe is ignoring you, or worse yet out to get you, you need to look for a cross purpose.

A cross purpose is when you think one thing, but you believe something completely different. Example: You may want money to flow to you, but you secretly believe that anytime something good happens "The other shoe must be about to drop." If that is the case, you will subconsciously be expecting something bad to happen. That means that all your energy will be going toward looking for the bad that is coming. And since that is where your energy will be focused, you will make something bad happen.

I have a friend, Donna, who has been struggling with something in her relationship. She has had a very hard time dealing with something her boyfriend does repeatedly that violates her boundaries. For several months I have heard her complain about this thing and the fact that it never changes. One day during a conversation, she had finally had enough of this behavior. She came to a point where she was done tolerating this behavior in her life. She was so firm in her conviction, that once the decision had been made, her boyfriend's behavior changed. She did not talk to him about it, nor did she communicate it to him in any way. The simple fact that she finally decided that it would not happen to her again, changed her reality. That is how powerful your thoughts and convictions are. They can literally change your reality in an instant.

Spirits and entities like to play and joke with us, and sometimes they affect us on a physical level. Just like people, not all energy beings are good or nice. It is very important to set a boundary around physical contact. You must be clear about NO TOUCHING at all. This includes nudging, tripping, poking, hair pulling, pushing, brushing, scratching etc. You can outline each item if that feels right to you, or just state no touching of any kind. As long as you are clear on your boundary the message will be sent.

Just like energy, dealing with the spirit world should not hurt in any way shape or form. You have every right to expect that you be treated well energetically. You also have the right to banish any spirit who refuses to play by your rules. Just remember that you are in charge. You have full control of your reality. Many people do not think about this need for separation, or the fact that you can ask for it. Again, the only limitations to what you can ask for are in your head.

I know a prevalent medium who suffered the first few times a being took over her body.

In Spiritism and Spiritualism the Channel or Medium has the role of an intermediary between the world of the living and the world of spirit. Mediums claim that they can listen to and relay messages from spirits, or that they can allow a spirit to control their body and speak through it directly or by using automatic writing or drawing. Spiritualists classify types of mediumship into two main categories: "mental" and "physical":

This particular Medium's soul was pushed aside so that the spirit could communicate with the audience. She recalls that the first few times it happened, once the channeling was done, she came back into her body and was violently ill from the experience. She rightfully set a boundary with her guides and other helpful spirits. If they wanted to communicate through her, they would have to do it alongside her. They were not allowed to push her out of the way. They would have to work with her and leave her in good shape, or not do it at all. If they were not ok with that, they would have to find another host.

Since then, she has had many years of successful channeling, and has never felt badly again. We are not at the mercy of the spirit world. They know that if they want to work with us, they must follow our rules, and they willingly comply. *We* are autonomous, powerful beings, and have the power to control how our energy is used. This is just like dealing with other humans. You get to decide who you work with, and under what circumstances.

One of my biggest rules, aside from no touching, is that anyone who is not willing to identify themselves or speak to me must leave immediately. They are not welcome near me, or in my space, until they are ready to communicate with me in a way that I understand. I have found that just like with people, friendly beings are more than happy to introduce themselves politely. Therefore, if you are not willing to be polite and tell me who you are, I am not willing to entertain you. It is very possible that when I set up this rule for myself I was not yet able to connect on a level which would allow me to clearly understand those who wished to connect with me. This was irrelevant as far as I was concerned. I have found that benevolent energies will respect the rule and help when they could. They would also keep trying to connect, and use different approaches.

When your vibration starts to rise, it is like turning on a flashing neon sign above your head. Everyone can see it, and they are all drawn to it. The nastier side involves entities that attach to you and make you feel bad. This can be emotional, physical or psychological negativity. You can start to feel sick, or cranky for no reason. You may become depressed and feel isolated from the world. What happens is that their energy starts attacking your energy body. It is like catching a flu. You start fighting it off, but since it is attached to you, it takes more than just a basic unconscious self-defense. You need to actively remove these beings.

There is a common misperception that spirits stay in one place and haunt it forever. That is not true. Many like to move around and will happily attach to anyone who is available and follow them home. As such, it is important to make sure that they know they may not follow you home just because they feel like it. It is a good idea to clear yourself of these "hitchhikers" before getting into a car, or getting home. Worst case, if you forget during the day, you can always announce at the end of the day that anyone who followed you home must leave immediately as they are not welcome.

These spirits are different from your guides because guides are part of your divine team. Like a football team, they are on your side and always with you. These hitchhikers are kind of like the crazy fan who decided they will jump on the team bus and hang out with the team. You can also set a perimeter around your house which will prevent anyone who does not have your explicit permission from entering. You do this by visualizing a white light around the area that you want to protect, and declaring that only those beings that have your permission to enter may do so. You can also set specific rules like "Only those people who honor, respect, love and understand me may enter." Or "Everyone who enters here must raise their vibration to match mine." Etc.

You can do this for your car as well. All you need to do is surround your home, car, etc. with a ball of white light.

You imagine the white light in your mind. Some people see it as a white light, some see it as a gold liquid flowing down, some can't see it at all so just imagine it there. No matter how it shows up for you, it is fine. And ask that it stay up permanently, and prevent anyone who does not belong from entering your space. I have actually found this quite helpful for humans too. I surrounded my car and apartment with a ball of while light and declared that only those who love, respect and honor me may enter my space. I can honestly say that it has worked at keeping me safe and feeling very secure. For several months I drove for Lyft and Uber.

I heard many crazy stories from other drivers about the people they got in their cars, and the interesting situations in which they found themselves. I never once had anyone strange, dangerous, mean or nasty get in my car. I never had any of those crazy stories. I fully believe that my barrier of protection was working for me, even though I never really thought about it. I set it once with a very solid intention, and then forgot about it. Worked like a charm.

Energy Should Not Hurt

No matter what you are going through, it is completely reasonable to ask that you are not negatively affected by the situation. You can ask your guides and helpers at any time to slow the process down+, or schedule major changes to happen when you are not awake. You should always be able to lead a semi-normal if not completely normal day. OR at least as normal as you can get under these circumstances. Not all days will be completely amazing, but you do not need to suffer at any point during this process. If you are suffering, it is because you want to be. Some people need the pain and struggle to know it is working, or because they need a bit of drama to feel alive. I was one of them for a while.

I had been hearing from many people, that we could and should ask our guides to adjust the speed of energy downloads, and ease up on the processing and energy shifts they were putting me through. Especially if it prevented me from functioning and being able to live a normal life. By doing this you will still get all the downloads and energy, but it will be gentle and less painful. You will be able to function. The problem was that I was a "push through and let it come as fast as possible" kind of girl.

I figured I will deal with it somehow, just get me through this process so I could come out on the other side and move on with my life. What I did not realize is that once this journey starts, it is continuous. It will go on forever. Once you decide to wake up spiritually, you allow yourself to start growing. This means that you will be growing perpetually.

You may as well relax and enjoy the ride. There is no end. It does get easier as you go, but this is a journey which keeps going. The hard part is the beginning because that is when you are removing all the physical and energetic toxins which are holding you in a lower vibration, and getting adjusted to the shifts and how they feel.

We have all heard of those people who live in haunted houses and are constantly under attack. The ghosts scratch them, or beat them up, or throw them against walls. The kinds of stories you think are made up until you start to deal with this world. Those people stay there thinking that in order to connect with the other dimensions you must feel it, and you must accept whatever abuse comes your way. They think that it is not truly happening if they can't experience it viscerally. I was definitely one of these people. As my ascension path started to unfold ahead of me I wanted to feel it. I needed to feel it. I thought that if I did not feel every moment of it, it must not be happening. My year had been very hard. I would wake up in the middle of the night overheated.

I went for a couple months barely getting sleep. I was irritable and cranky. There were the few weeks when my body decided that all I was allowed to eat was a very specific type of food. I was only allowed to eat at certain times during the day. I was having severe mood swings all the time. I would wake up happy and full of energy, then by noon I was depressed and exhausted. I could never tell where my day was going and how I would feel. As you can imagine, this caused problems with being around people. It also caused problems being with myself. No sane, rational person wants to inflict that kind of craziness on strangers, let alone their friends. Because of this, I had become very isolated.

Although I had people telling me that it was OK to ask my guides to slow things down, that there was nothing wrong with having them back off and letting it take a bit longer, to me, this seemed crazy. I had made a decision and was going to push full steam ahead until it was done. I wanted this crazy ascension pain to go quickly, and then be done. The only caveats I put on it was that it could not impair me medically in any way, and I was to come out the other side fully functional in every way. Other than that, my guides were to push as hard and fast as they could. I was ready to get it over with.

That thought process was great for about a year. If I am to be completely honest, it should have ended after about a week. One day I woke up and realized that I was no longer living life. I was existing in my body, and had no idea for what. It had been a hard year, and not one that I had much to show for. It was at that moment that I decided NO MORE!! Energy should not hurt.

There was no reason that I had to accept pain along with the wonderful gifts that were coming my way. It happened to be a morning when I woke up happy and full of life. I had had enough and was ready to get back to living. I had a very serious conversation with my guides. This is easily done. All you have to do is imagine them there in the room with you, assuming you cannot see them. They are always around as they are there to help you, so they will hear and listen when you talk. Just because you cannot hear or see them does not mean the reverse is true.

I explained that although I was all in with the ascension process, I was no longer willing to accept pain in any form along with it. I was clear on the specific feelings that I was expecting to experience every day. I pointed to the exact way I felt right then and told them that they may give me all the gifts they want, and all the shifting that needs to happen as fast as they want, but I was to feel as alive and happy as I did at that moment at all times. I definitely thanked them for all the work they were doing, and made it clear that I was grateful and happy with where I was going.

It was my decision to come here to experience this life, and along with those experiences remember my gifts. Part of using my gifts was creating a life that felt good. Given that I had decided to be here and alive, I was clear on the fact that this experience was not to be thrown away on something that could happen pain free. It was time to start living again. Since that day I have had the most marvelous experience. I am happy and actually enjoying life. I definitely feel and sense the gifts that are coming my way as they are very clear. I have started an abundant flow which was bringing all sorts of wonderful presents to me. My phone has been ringing off the hook with customers who were referred to me. My business has started to thrive. I had been asking for my business to go international, and I have now reached people in multiple countries.

Mentors

You will need mentors, and people with whom you can talk about this. This journey is interesting, challenging, hard at times and frankly sounds crazy to people who are not on this path. You need to find some people with whom you can discuss what you are going through. You also need to find mentors who can guide you along. Just like with any new skill you want to develop, it is always helpful to have people who are further along the journey than you. When something happens, someone can tell you what it means, or what is going on, or perhaps why it is happening. If nothing else, they can lend a sympathetic, understanding ear. They have gone through that stage already and can share their wisdom with you. Be sure that the people you choose as your mentors are worthy of that role. Don't choose someone you hardly know and don't trust. If you trust your instincts, you will know who to turn to for help. The right people will always show up if you are open to their help.

During the first stages of this journey I had given up my power to every human I met who it seemed to me already had the abilities that I was seeking. I had been in such a crazed hurry to reach the end that I just listened to everyone's "expert advice". I wanted the powers and wanted them now. I sought out mentors who knew more than I did, or so I thought. I looked at anyone who was "psychic", or rather claimed to be psychic, as better than me. Clearly they had what I wanted, so they must be the people who would get me where I needed to go. At least I thought they had what I wanted.

Many times it turned out that they had no idea what they were talking about. The problem was that I had no faith in my own intuition, so I just blindly followed anyone who claimed to do what I wanted to do. I would hang on every word they said, and do whatever they told me. I never stopped to question their advice against my own truth. Frankly, sometimes I did things that didn't feel amazing, but figured "They must know, so who am I to question?" I asked them questions about how to become better. I would ignore my own intuition and knowledge, and replace it with their advice. I would not bother to form my own opinion or consider if I already knew the answer. I treated them as if they were the all-knowing authority, and I was someone who would never achieve their level of success. Basically I put them on a pedestal and followed blindly.

There is an inherent danger in this thought process, I'm sure you are already seeing it. It is, however, a very common occurrence. Many people fall into this trap. Many very intelligent and capable people. If that is you, it is OK, you are not alone. The problem was that although the people I was following were indeed more advanced than I, they did not necessarily know what was right for me. Their advice was coming from what was right for them at that particular stage in their journey. I did not see the journey as possible without some external force. I thought that I needed someone else to make it happen. I was expecting to hop in a cab and let someone else drive me to the final destination. I was still unwilling to see that I had to find my own car, learn how to drive, and actually drive myself there using my own maps.

They had practiced the things I refused to, or rather the things that I didn't know how to do. I kept hearing "You need to stop and meditate. You need to listen within." My challenge with this was that I can't meditate. My brain will not shut down long enough to do so. How was I supposed to do something that I can't? Turns out there are many ways to meditate. Sitting still and chanting was just one of them. Walking in nature quietly is another. Vacuuming, washing dishes, sewing, etc. Anything that quiets the left / logical half of your brain so that the right one can go to work. For me, staring at a water fountain works wonders. The left side of my brain can latch on to the patterns of the water, so that it quiets down. Once the left brain shuts off, the right brain kicks on, and that is when the magic starts to happen. Figure out what works for you and use that. Forget how everyone else does it.

When I had gotten everything I could from one teacher, I would seek out the next, then the next. I would spend hours looking for articles, lectures, manuals, hoping for the one that would give me the easy button. I took classes and spent money on personal sessions hoping for the one cab driver who would just take me where I wanted to go. I was searching for that one little thing that I could do which would open up all my abilities. There is nothing wrong with seeking mentors. That is how you learn. But I had fallen into a trap which is common amongst those who are working to gain a new skill set. It is a human thing. In this journey, it is very easy to want to learn the logical left brained way in which we learn everything else. Give me the information, and the steps to take, let me take the steps and I will just get there. I start at point A, I walk this line and, voila, I arrive at point B.

We want someone to show us, then we do what they did, then we know and have mastered the task. That does not work with this process. This process involves opening up the right side of the brain, and looking to yourself as the teacher. It involves understanding that you are the holder of all the wisdom, and don't need anyone else to give you anything. Your intuition is your psychic gift. Once you learn to connect to it, and trust what it is telling you, you will arrive. The challenge is that getting there is not linear. It involves winding roads, releasing toxicity from your life, cleaning out your energy body, and realigning with a set of mental "muscles" that you more than likely shut off a long time ago. It involves your brain shifting its way of thinking to a whole new process. This alone takes time since you need to get there slowly as your hormonal and physical shifts must accompany the energetic ones. Some people have gone crazy from shifting too fast. Imagine one day waking up being able to see inside people's bodies while having dramatic mood swings. Your brain would not know how to deal with that and may shut down. That is ultimately what any good mentor will guide you to know.

It took a series of mentors disappearing from my life to show me this fact. In essence, I was forced into a sort of isolation. Around the time when I started truly connecting with my higher self and my own knowing, my mentors, the people I was looking to for guidance stopped being available. It was almost as if they fell off the face of the earth. They would not respond to my online messages or texts. No returned calls. Nothing. I felt as if I had been set adrift in a vast ocean and there was no help in sight. At one point I had messaged a mentor with a question. After several days she had not responded, so I sent a second message asking if she was okay. She responded with "Yes."

I followed up by telling her I had been worried about her because she usually responded. Her response was "I don't respond to left brain questions." Essentially telling me to stop with the linear thinking and start going with guidance. This was not a mean spirited thing. She was doing this to several people, as her students confirmed since we were still talking to each other looking for answers. It was her way of forcing me to start trusting my own guidance and stop asking other people for the answers that I already had. I needed to connect with my own personal power and internal knowing.

A good mentor will never abandon you or tell you that you need to figure it out on your own. I have dealt with many people who would not answer questions or help when I was struggling. They would tell me that everyone has a different experience so answering my question would be futile because it was my own journey. Let me say right now, that response is a bunch of BULL. Although each person goes through their own version of the symptoms, there are many commonalities. So many in fact, that hand-holding is easy. They would tell me to ask myself, because I already had the answers. If you have a mentor like this, seriously consider finding a new one. Unless you happen to appreciate this approach. I personally have not met anyone who does.

That kind of answer is sufficient for someone who is truly ready for the task and just not getting there on their own, but it should never happen at the beginning of the process. That would be like a Karate teacher telling a yellow belt to go ahead and fight the street gang, because they already had a couple lessons so they must be ready. A good mentor will be there with you until you can truly do it alone. And even then, they will not abandon you. If you are truly struggling, they will happily come to your aid. Although my mentor told me that she would no longer answer left brain questions, she was more than happy to help if I said "I am hearing this, but it does not sound right. What is the message really?" Be very wary of anyone who gives you a couple tips then stops having time to help you out. They are not a good mentor. Find another.

It was in this void where I started seeing my own power. It was in this void where I had no choice but to listen to my own intuition. Ask myself a question and trust the answer that came up. Start trusting my gut. Start going with the flow, no matter where it led me. Know that if I was headed in one direction and it felt bad I needed to turn around immediately.

I needed to stop second guessing my own hunches and stop thinking "Oh, that is just my imagination, it doesn't mean anything." When I started to realize that I actually had the power that I was looking to others for, I started attracting people who were just starting on this path themselves. They were asking ME questions about what happens. They were looking to ME as the expert. This realization was a bit of a mind bender. In a very short time I had gone from begging for information, to being the expert. And actually having the answers they were seeking.

At this point I really started looking within myself. I started asking myself questions (any question I wanted) and getting the answers I needed. I started having faith in my internal knowledge. I started trusting my own guidance and seeing it as valid, more valid that the knowledge and answers that I was getting from others. I had no problem rejecting information or advice if it did not fully resonate with me regardless of the knowledge level of the person who was delivering the advice. I started trusting in the fact that I had all the "Super Powers" I needed, and had been seeking all along. I realized that as I was doing a healing session, I was seeing, feeling, knowing, and channeling just like all those mentors who I had been looking up to. I was just as good. My barrier to growth had been my expectations. I was expecting to see a sexy romantic version of a perfect life as a psychic who had random ghosts come out of nowhere and give me answers. I expected them to hand me information for other people so that I could just walk up to them and tell them all about their lives, and that was not what I was getting.

What I was getting was very powerful and clear, but because it did not line up with what I was expecting, I was rejecting it as invalid exactly like I did with my Cow guide. I suppose I should find out her name at some point. I have not done that yet. In case you are wondering, this is completely fine, and not disrespectful at all. There are guides who come and go as they are needed. It is not always easy to connect with them to find out their names. What is important is that they are acknowledged and their help is respected.

Interacting with Energy

I made it through the big, bad, ugly part of the journey, and have come out the other side. This does not mean that I am no longer experiencing those weird symptoms. They still happen, but less frequently, less severely, and I now know what is happening and can work with it. It was time to start working on other people. I was ready and started drawing people and experiences to me which would help me learn further. This next part is about some of the valuable lessons I learned while doing healing work on others. This will be good information to keep in the back of your mind if you decide to work on people energetically. These lessons and experiences are harder to find documented as they are taught to medicine people, and those who are very advanced with the Light worker skills. I believe they are very important to know for anyone who will be working on others. I am not telling these stories as an example of a typical or even common occurrence. These are truly rare events, but so many things happened to me at once, that I find it to be a good example of many things to be aware of. The reality is that most healing sessions are calm, relaxing and everything goes well. Clients are often very receptive and happy when it is done.

Some people have such elaborate subconscious defense systems in place protecting their energy that they have set up guardians to hurt anyone who makes it through their other defenses. I had heard about this, and thought it was interesting, but did not understand what it meant until I worked on someone like this. She was very angry and defensive, and had set up just these kinds of barriers around herself. The first thing I always do with any client is get their permission to work on them. This can either come from them consciously stating that it is OK out loud, or from their higher self.

You do this by connecting to their higher self and asking permission. If you do not get this permission, there is a good chance that you will not be able to work on them as they will block you. With this particular lady I had gotten her verbal permission, and she seemed eager for the session.

About 5 minutes after I started my hands began hurting. It was an internal pain like a strong electric current moving up my hands and arms. I stopped working on her and asked her to give me permission to continue. That neutralized the first layer of defenses. The next thing I encountered were her guardians. What I saw psychically was an animal with the body of an alligator and two lion heads rushing at me. I removed my hands and stepped back. I asked if she wanted to continue and she said yes. So I asked her to tell her guardians that I have permission to be here and work on her. I made her do this out loud. When I started working on her again. Again the guardian started running toward me to attack. I mentally looked straight at it and told it that I had permission to be here. Like all guides and guardians it listened and stopped. I was then able to continue working on her for a while longer.

The final thing that happened in this session was that part of her defenses, or some entity that was around her decided to attack me fully. I started shaking, feeling queasy and my body started hurting. I immediately stopped the work and moved off to the side. A mentor of mine who was in the room saw what was happening and took me in to one of our empty offices for some clearing. I felt so bad that I had to sit down on the floor so I wouldn't fall as she was working on me.

After about 3 minutes I solidified the final, and very important piece of my education. *I am in charge.* I have complete power over my energy field. I get to decide who and what comes in and how long they stay. I immediately connected to the Universe and started pulling in the Light. The same Light that has been referenced before. I watched it come in to my heart and fill it up. From there I created an energy ball which expanded out from my heart to surround both me and my mentor, and remove whatever was attacking me from the building. I saw and felt it happening. The moment I kicked out the offending entity my mentor said it was done. She asked if I had felt it leave. I started laughing because I had done it. I had taken full control of my energy field. Never forget that you are in control of your energy field and can remove anything at any time.

I also want to discuss working on people and some basic rules that any good healer, empath, channel, light worker, etc. should follow. It is very important that if you receive a message during a session while you are working on someone, whether it comes as words, pictures, feelings, or any other way, you do not give it meaning. The message should be delivered exactly as you got it. The problem with not doing so is that any meaning you give it will apply to you, not your client. If you see a rose, you should tell the person "I see a rose, does that mean anything to you?"

The reason for this is that any translation you put on something must first go through your filter. This automatically changes the message because you do not have the client's experience and memories. Example: I was working with a lady and saw a rose bud. My interpretation would have been that she was a beautiful soul and at the start of her journey. Turns out that her middle name was Rose. The message was very powerful and important, but would have lost all meaning had I tried to translate. This also showed her that I was actually receiving relevant information.

Many people are skeptical about "messages from beyond" because they worked with people who passed on interpretations. Of course the messages meant nothing to the client. By the time the message was delivered it had been altered completely. Many people have also been scarred by psychics who put their own spin on a message and passed along doom and gloom prophecies.

I know a man who has had a horrible life and is very angry at the world. As a child he suffered some form of abuse. He is also fairly open energetically. In his youth he worked with a mentor who was a psychic. This person gave him a very bad reading that foretold darkness and unhappiness through the rest of his life. To this day he is living out his resistance to that reading, and creating all kinds of bad occurrences in his life.

He put so much faith in that person that he took on the reading as his identity. He is not able to see another way. I spoke with him and tried to explain that what that person had told him was not gospel. That is the problems with passing along interpretations rather than the exact message. He agreed, but his subconscious could not let the information go. These are the kind of thing that can happen when you pass along what you think rather than what you get.

You Have

All You Need

It was not always fair. I had wanted the full psychic gamut for a long time. I wanted to see and talk to spirits. Talk to angels, have God come in the room and work through me, make magic happen, etc. Basically, if it was a psychic tool in the quiver, I wanted it. I remember going to a class with one of my mentors where she told us about one of her recent students. She had been working with this student for a short while, and the lady "opened up." She was now able to see and talk to spirits and do the things that I wanted to do. After this had happened, the lady had started to complain. The spirits were showing up everywhere, and talking to her and asking for help. Apparently she did not want those abilities, and wanted to "turn it off" because she had changed her mind and no longer wanted what she had.

I was completely jealous and upset at the same time. Here was this woman, who had been asking for and subsequently gifted with the things that I wanted. And she wanted to return the gift. What? I asked if we could just transfer it over to me. I would happily take her castoffs. No reason for them to go to waste. Why not? The gifts need to go somewhere, so why not the person who would actually value them. Apparently that is not how it works. It was not my path to connect with the spirits in the way she had, so that power could not shift my way.

After a while I started thinking, was that really a bad thing? I don't walk into rooms and see random people who should not be there staring at me. I don't wake up in the middle of the night seeing strangers standing over my bed because they need to talk to someone. I am able to have conversations without weird paranormal stuff interrupting. I can go to the bathroom, take a shower, and do all the sorts of other private things without seeing someone else watching me. No, it was not a bad thing at all.

While it would definitely be fun to have all the "fun" parlor tricks out there, perhaps it was for the best that I was not granted those particular gifts. I have realized that I am much more powerful than I had thought. Those tricks would not give me power, they would only give me the illusion of power. My real gifts became obvious when I saw myself and my gifts as enough. I also know that my gifts are not limited to what they are today. This whole time, they have been growing and increasing in strength.

When I first started I was only able to feel energy in my hands as heat. Now I can see messages in the form of movies. I can hear guidance as it comes through. I have been able to channel on occasion. I physically feel when someone has a physical problem and I know exactly what it is and where it came from. When this happens I can actually feel the problem physically in my own body. If their neck hurts, mine will hurt. If their ankle hurts, mine will start to hurt as well. I also somehow say things to people which they need to hear. I will be in a conversation with someone and the most random things will come out. Many times those random things will be exactly what that person needed to hear at that moment.

No, I can't see spirits or ghosts, but I have more than I need to function in the energetic world. And so do you.

Symptom list

1. High degree of stress, anxiety – but no apparent reason for this – New energy coming in and pushing old – patterns, beliefs, behaviors to the surface for release.
2. Extreme exhaustion/fatigue – due to our bodies transforming into a crystalline structure to reside in higher dimension – becoming less dense – this takes an incredible amount of energy
3. Adrenal stress, blowout or fatigue – may be occuring at varying degrees depending upon where you are on your journey, how you run and process energy and stress, sleep you are getting and foods you are eating.
4. Sleeplessness
5. Inability to wake up or periods of deep sleeping – rest period after a lot of energy has come in, preparing for another period of intense inflow of energy, processing another leap in expansion or vibratioin
6. Waking up at odd hours – or waking up at the same time on the clock each night
7. Neck pain/stiffness
8. Foot pain, lower leg pain, stiffness and aching – 'old man syndrome' – i.e., feeling the need to shuffle along while you walk or barely able to walk or move – all due to grounding onto the new earth and taking in the new energies into the body via the feet and legs
9. Low and midback pain and discomfort – sometimes severe – often between the shoulder blades – also known as 'sprouting the angel wings'
10. Night sweats/hot flashes – mock menopause, burning off the lower and denser aspects of ourselves and dark energies
11. Feeling cold with inability to get warm
12. Sinus pressure/headaches/migraines and lots of congestion –

13. opening of crown chakra to allow intake of more energy and greater connection to higher realms, activation of pineal and pituitary glands to increase intuitive and psychic abilities
14. Joint and muscle aches, pain and stiffness
15. Loss of memory – short term – what did I just do, say, eat, read, can't remember appointments, commitments, etc. – longer term – can't remember what you did, said, wore last week or last month.
16. Lack of ability to concentrate/lack of focus
17. Loss of appetite
18. OR Feeling ravenous/hungry all the time or at certain times
19. craving for sweets
20. Need to eat often – craving for protein
21. Weight gain – abdominal area – need to expand our being to carry more weight as we are becoming so light we need to ground ourselves on the earth and not float away – also a way to create a layer of "protection" so to speak around our power charkas – from the lower vibrating energies when we interact with them
22. OR weight loss – no longer need to "hold on" to extra weight or our bodies have adapted to the expansion and so do not need to be literally bigger to hold more light – can do it energetically.
23. Digestive/digestive tract issues – constipation, loose stool, stomach upset/discomfort/pain, bloating and indigestion, inability to properly digest food – due to your vibration and the vibration of the food you are consuming no longer aligning, the cleansing and clearing out of your system of all lower vibrating 'poop' you have been carrying around – physically, mentally, emotionally and spiritually, as well as preparation of you 'Gut' to begin to take on the role of the 'Golden Stove' or area of purification where you can literally cleanse yourself from any dark, toxic or negative energies that may be experienced either externally in your environements or created internally by you

24. Tastes in food change – for example you may notice you lose a taste for and stop eating meat
25. Eating certain kinds of foods – particularly processed and foods with high amounts of sugar (even natural sugar), salt and fat – causes you to shake – inside and out
26. Allergies – new ones develop or acting up of current or old ones
27. Strange rashes
28. Itchy skin – sometimes feels like something crawling on your skin
29. Intermittent muscle twitching – in limbs, fingers, etc.
30. Heart pain and palpitations – feels like your heart is racing – acclimating to higher and more intense energies, opening and activating of heart chakra
31. Difficulty breathing – difficult to take a deep breath or like you can't catch your breath
32. Blurred vision – seeing with new eyes in the new vibration, inability to see what is next or see your truth or true self as it emerges
33. Dizziness/Vertigo/Loss of Balance
34. Feeling out of body, not grounded, not present, untethered, spacey , not 'here' anymore – walking between two worlds or dimensions or in new dimension and not fully present to it
35. Ringing in the ears
36. Loss of ability to (remember how to) write/write certain words/spell/speak and even comprehend – due to jumping back and forth between dimensions, disconnect – not aligned with time – part of you is here and part of you has jumped to the other dimension
37. Heightened sensitivity to sound, light and smell, energies around you – tuning up your frequency/vibration
38. Things no longer sounding normal – have a 'tinny', hollow or strange sound to them
39. "Ascension Flu"
40. Buzzing, Vibrating sensation or feeling of electricity moving through your body – new and higher energies being taken in to the body, process of expansion,

activation of chakras, solar discs, your solar light body and shifting of your DNA
41. Hair turning gray or white in a localized spot on your head – for example a dollarsized spot appearing at the crown
42. Sensitivity to heat and sun
43. Sensitivity to your environment/surroundings/the energies in those surroundings

2. Emotional:

1. Depression – clearing out negative lower vibrating energies
2. Panic
3. Anxiety
4. Confusion
5. Lack of Clarity
6. Fear, terror
7. Feelings of hysteria
8. Suicidal
9. Weeping
10. Apathy – feeling blah
11. Sometimes feeling nothing at all – in a place of no feeling – can be disconcerting but this is a clear space and often comes just before or after a major transition point and before we put our human/ego labels on or in to what we are feeling or should be feeling – this is not the same as numb or disassociated/disconnected
12. Feeling of emptiness – another form of this no feeling or nothingness – feeling nothing – no thing and often comes with desire to immediately fill oneself up – usually with food – sugar – or with tasks – "doingness"
13. Restlessness
14. Strong emotional ups and downs
15. Wild, sometimes violent and vivid dreams
16. Lack of motivation or ambition – just don't feel like doing anything at all – we are in a period of rest – we are realigning – this is part of being in the New Vibration or higher dimensions as needing to make

things happen or in the 'doing' state is no longer necessary – we are squarely in the state of 'BE'ing

3. Mental/Psychological:

1. Loss of identity – releasing of the ego self/facets and human form – connecting more to soul or higher self and Godsource
2. Lack of purpose
3. Loss of motivation, drive, ambition
4. Not knowing what you like anymore – with respect to things, jobs, people, even your taste in food, style of clothing, etc.
5. Loss of self
6. Lots of losses or disappearance of – job, money, relationships, health, family members/friends, – moving beyond what no longer aligns with our vibration – needing to clear out or clear away what no longer vibrates at the same frequency in order to move on or up to next level
7. Feeling of loss of entire support structure
8. Feeling the absolute 'End' of things is here or that things are 'over' or the energy is just dead and you don't have the ability to or interest in reinvigorating them – for example, relationships/friendships, unsatisfying jobs, where you live, how you have typically have done things or operated in your life, what you think, feel believe, etc.
9. Inability to find or remember words for things, forget what you were saying in the middle of your sentence,
10. Basically feeling like you are going crazy

4. Spiritual/Vibrational/Energetic:

1. Feeling of emptying out or being emptied out or clearing out
2. Religious beliefs may change or break down or fall away
3. Morals and values may be thrown into question

4. Ego bucks, pushes back as it releases and makes way for the soul wisdom to step forward
5. Disconnection from any structured sense of Time – don't know what time it is – no relationship to it, forget/miss appointments, can't keep track of time and no desire to or to be constrained by it, sense of being in timeless space or stuck in time, sense of time racing by – due to now being in the time of no time or timelessness
6. Letting go of being Egocentric and living from the head governed by logical/practical thinking and 'doingness'
7. 'Disconnects' and breakdowns begin to occur everywhere in your life: with relationships and people – old friends fall away or move out of your life suddenly or you may end a marriage or partnership; with circumstances and situations – you may leave or lose a job that is no longer a vibrational match or in alignment with your current frequency or you may move from your current location; and with technology
8. you may experience technical issues with your computer or cell phone – you may find they go off line, can't find a signal or simply melt down; your landline may have static when you speak with people who do not hold the same energetic space; you may experience computers going down or operating very slowly when you are in the vicinty – like in a store or when you call a customer support line; batteries drain more quickly – e.g., fire or CO_2 detectors, flashlights, cellphones, etc.; other electronic devices or electrical machinery begin breaking down or burning out – all of this due to both your own increasing vibration and the inability of the frequency of who and what is around you to align and/or keep up.

5. Other:

1. Sudden change/s occurring – big and small – that can cause major upheaval if we are not grounded – e.g., change/s in plans in general – or specifically everywhere in life – at work, with projects, in relationship status/marriage/friendships, with clients, where we live, our health, etc.
2. No desire to wear jewelry – or a feeling of constriction when wearing it
3. Tastes change – taste in food, clothes, furniture, style etc.

6. Positive Symptoms!

1. Heightened awareness
2. Intuition opens and deepens – more in touch with heart – can hear own truth, can read situations with increased perception, clarity and knowing, psychic abilities also open or enhance
3. At a certain point – more willing to listen to self and trust self
4. Start to look younger – and feel younger
5. Experience spontaneous healings – of both new and longstanding ailments
6. Loss of fear of death/dying
7. Releasing/Loss of ego – healing of past wounds
8. Getting off wheel of karma – completing our past
9. Being unattached to outcomes or results
10. Less focus on ego's concerns – money, worries, "what ifs" – the deeper soul knowing takes over and trusts all is well –you're your higher voice tells you these concerns aren't really important anyway as you will have evolved beyond them in the New vibration
11. More focused on what is REALLY important in life
12. Start to follow path of Soul Purpose and calling
13. Willing to take more risks regardless of external circumstances and fear
14. Take on or seek a slower pace of life

15. More internally focused and inspired than externally driven
16. Move away from isolated individual and competitiveness to unity and collaboration with others
17. Living in the Now moment and being Present based
18. Now living fully from the Heart governed by Heart Wisdom, intuitive/energetic sensing and 'BE'ingness
19. Able to manifest immediately what is most desired and aligns with highest and best good and is in the interests of highest and best good of all
20. Easing of these symptoms as you move through this process and a renewed energy emerging
21. More attunement, comfort with and trust of the Intuition and 'gut'/Heart based decision making and processing
22. Prosperity, Abundance and Flow are effortlessly available if we can remain in the Now Moment and keep our vibration pure.

(Harris, 2010)

References

Beckwith, M. B. (2008). life visioning [Recorded by M. B. Beckwith].

Emoto, M. (2010, January 1). *Office Masaru Emoto*. Retrieved from www.masaru-emoto.net: http://www.masaru-emoto.net/english/water-crystal.html.

Harris, H. (2010, January 1). *Ascension-Symptoms*. Retrieved from ascension 360: http://www.ascension360.net/resources-2/ascension-symptoms/

Hawkins, D. R. (1995). Frequency Spectrum. In D. R. Hawkins, *Power vs. Force*. Sedona: Veritas Publishing.

Science, W. I. (1998, February 27). *ScienceDaily*. Retrieved from Science Daily: https://www.sciencedaily.com/releases/1998/02/980227055013.htm

Shamay, S. (2016, May 23). Editing Notes. (K. Shamay, Interviewer)

Stibal, V. (2016). *www.thetahealing.com*. Retrieved from Theta Healing spiritual, physical, emotional well being: http://www.thetahealing.com/about-thetahealing/thetahealing-theta-state.html

Keren Shamay

TAMT, EFTMP, METAP, Dr. Metaphysics
keren@kerenshamay.com
www.kerenshamay.com/energyworkcoaching

.

www.ingramcontent.com/pod-product-compliance
Lightning Source LLC
Chambersburg PA
CBHW060551100426
42742CB00013B/2514